ORIENTEERING
The Skills of the Game

ORIENTEERING

The Skills of the Game

CAROL McNEILL

THE CROWOOD PRESS

First Published in 1989 by
The Crowood Press
Ramsbury, Marlborough
Wiltshire SN8 2HE

British Library Cataloguing in Publication Data

McNeill, Carol
    Orienteering: the skills of the game.
    1. Orienteering
    I. Title
    796.5

    ISBN 1 – 85223 – 151 – 3

Dedicated to my Mother

Acknowledgements
Special thanks to Ann McNeill for checking the script, my sister Hilary
Cochrane for typing it, Allan Mason for never-ending patience and
support, and everyone in orienteering who helped me along the road.

Thanks also to photographers Stuart Parker for the cover photograph and
Figs 1, 72, 82, 89 and 94, David Briggs for Figs 87, 122, 126, 129, 136
and 137 and Jonathon Taylor for all the other photographs.

Further thanks to Harveys for map symbols and international descriptions,
Rob Bloor for the training diary, Silva UK for compasses, and the
following for providing maps: Octavian Droobers, Lakeland OC, SOA,
BOF, Birmingham City Leisure, Walton Chasers, Solway OC, Forth Valley
Orienteers, Chigwell OC, SEOA, Interlopers, Harlequins OC, YMCA
Lakeside, Dudley Leisure Services.

Line illustrations by Clare Upsdale-Jones

Note: throughout this book, the pronouns 'he', 'him' and 'his' are intended
to apply both to men and women. It is important in sport, as elsewhere,
that women and men should have equal status and opportunities.

Typeset by Mayhew Typesetting
Printed in Great Britain by the Bath Press

Contents

I was introduced to orienteering by Chris Brasher back in the mid-sixties and like many climbers I was immediately captivated by the sense of adventure and the spur of competition – who said climbers aren't competitive? The ability to read a map gives you the freedom and confidence to explore new places, whether it is an unfamiliar city or one of the remaining wilderness areas of the world. Orienteering must be one of the fastest and most enjoyable ways to learn navigational skills as well as being a challenging and satisfying sport in its own right. Most important of all, it can be enjoyed to the full at every level, whether you are an international competitor going for the highest prize, or carrying an infant in a papoose on your back round one of the easier courses.

I've certainly learned a lot from Carol's book. She captures and passes on the fun of orienteering and yet packs in a mass of tips to help the beginner get started and the veteran to sharpen up his game. Use this book as a source of reference and I am sure that it will help you as it has helped me, either to take your first steps in this delightful sport or to get even more from your ventures with map and compass.

Chris Bonington
Mountaineer, Honorary President,
BOF

Carol McNeill has wide experience of teaching and coaching orienteering to all ages and levels of ability. Team Coach to the British squad in the 1984-85 World Championships, she is currently a selector and a coaching co-ordinator for the squad, and a Senior Coach with the British Orienteering Federation.

British Ladies' Champion five times, Carol is her country's most successful international competitor, achieving twelfth and seventh place in successive World Championships, and one gold and two bronze medals in the veterans' event. In 1984 she was awarded the MBE for her services to orienteering.

Carol is unique in British sport having reached the top both as competitor and coach. World-class competitors can seldom, if ever, explain how they got to those exalted heights while those who have the gift of teaching seldom, if ever, know what it feels like to take part in a world championship.

Over the past twenty years Carol has been a world-class competitor, beating many of the top Scandinavians and maintaining her status as British number one. As a coach of both the physical and the mental aspects of orienteering she is unsurpassed outside Scandinavia and I would have no hesitation in recommending her to any enthusiast. So go forth into the pages of this book with Carol and enjoy yourself. There is nobody I would rather have to guide me through the forests and hills.

Chris Brasher
Former Olympic athlete, Co-founder and Chairman,
British Orienteering Federation

Orienteering more than most sports is a struggle with self as well as opponents and its skills have to be learned systematically rather than by trial and error. Carol McNeill's experience as motivator and teacher for young and old makes her uniquely qualified to set both newcomer and ambitious convert on the right path. In the late sixties she was one of the pioneers of the sport and her achievements since have gained her world-wide respect. Her career is inseparable from the history of the sport in Britain.

In this book Carol leads the reader through a systematic but uncomplicated explanation of the techniques and training methods central to the sport. Along with thoughtful tips plucked from her unrivalled wealth of experience, there is throughout an emphasis on the fact that success ultimately depends on the reader's own determination and application. Like all lovers of the great outdoors, Carol prefers 'doing' to 'talking' and I am sure that the reader will find her company on the journey through this book as inspiring as I have found it.

Peter Palmer
Director of Coaching, BOF

Introduction

Orienteering is a running sport. The competitive orienteer runs with a map and compass, choosing his own way, to find a fixed number of control points which are marked very precisely on the map, and are indicated in the terrain by a large red and white control marker. At each control point a 'pin punch' is attached for each competitor to mark his or her control card and therefore prove that the control has been visited. A code number or letters, also fixed to the control, establishes that it is the correct control on the course. The course will vary between one and thirteen kilometres, with six to thirty control points. The distance and technical difficulty will depend on age, sex, experience and fitness. Within each class, it is the person finding all the controls in the right order in the shortest time who wins.

HISTORY

Orienteering was introduced to Britain in the early 1960s having already become well established as a sport in the Scandinavian countries. The Swedes were the pioneers. One of the first official events was organised by Major Ernst Killander in 1918 as a result of his concern for a falling interest in athletics and a lack of use of the forest environment. It has grown since then to become one of the most popular sports in Sweden. Many take part purely on a recreational basis, using the short courses set up each summer close to most towns. The Swedish annual 5-day O-Ringen Event reflects this popularity in attracting over 20,000 competitors in classes covering a wide age range from eight to eighty years old.

It was a Swede, Baron 'Rak' Lagerfelt who had a major influence in establishing the sport in Britain. The first orienteering clubs were formed by athletes with an interest in navigation, climbing and fell running. South Ribble Orienteering Club, Southern Navigators, and Edinburgh Southern Orienteering Club were the first of over 150 different clubs which now cover the whole of the United Kingdom.

The interest and organisational energy of well-established and international athletes such as John Disley, Chris Brasher, Bruce Tulloh, Martin Hyman, Gordon Pirie and Lancashire climber Gerry Charnley, helped

Fig 1   A pin punch at a control point.

7

a great deal in developing the sport in its early days, including the implementation of guidelines and rules of competition.

In 1967 the English and Scottish Orienteering Associations amalgamated to form the British Orienteering Federation. The BOF is the governing body of the sport which co-ordinates the administration and maintenance of standards through several committees which consist of representatives from all the twelve regions covering the British Isles. A full time professional officer – the General Secretary – ensures the smooth running of the sports administration through an office in Matlock, which also handles any enquiries about the sport. The more recent employment of a Director of Coaching, Peter Palmer, has had a positive effect on the development of coaching in clubs, and establishing orienteering as a valuable curriculum subject in schools. In 1987 there were 157 clubs spread throughout the country with a record 204,455 competitors at 1,312 events.

The growth of the sport has been largely influenced by the improvement in the quality of maps. The early events were dependent on copies of Ordnance Survey maps. Now, with advances in printing technology, most events are able to provide a specially drawn large-scale map in five colours for each competitor. The areas are surveyed and the map drawn by orienteers using internationally recognised drawing specifications. 5 metre or 2.5 metre contours show the precise shape of the terrain and other details such as large boulders, pits, gullies, depressions and small crags which enable the orienteer to know exactly where he is all the time, as well as provide a large number of potential control sites. The time-consuming job of making maps involving photogrammetry, surveying, cartography and printing is now available from a number of small businesses who offer this very specialist service. Susan and Robin Harvey, international orienteers themselves, pioneered this professional status in Britain, after committing themselves for two years to making the maps for the 1976 World Championships held near Forres in Scotland. Many clubs are also able to draw on the skills of members who have made mapmaking their spare time interest. Learning how to make maps is also good training for map interpretation if you are a competitor.

The sport is now established in over thirty countries. World Championships are held every two years, alternating with a prestigious World Cup series, both attracting athletes of high calibre. There are also World Student Championships, World Junior Championships for under-21s and a Veteran's World Cup for those over 35.

A SPORT FOR ALL

At its most competitive the sport offers a lot to the athlete who likes to think, as well as run. The sport is also organised to offer a challenge to children and adults of all ages and athletic ability. String courses for the under-tens allow even three or four-year-old children to enjoy running through woodland and finding controls, whilst classes for the veterans, in five year age groupings from thirty-five to seventy, give an opportunity for athletes and non-athletes alike to participate in a running sport at whatever level they choose. Walking round a course with accurate map reading may not put you at the top of your class but it certainly will not put you at the bottom. The story of the tortoise and the hare can be aptly applied to this sport.

Orienteering gives you confidence in handling a map and compass in any naviga-

Fig 2   String courses enable very young children to enjoy orienteering.

the structure of the organisation ensures that everyone starting out is accounted for at the end. The skills of orienteering have to be learned from the experience gained from many events and many mistakes. This book will help you maximise that experience and reduce the number of unnecessary mistakes. The chapters on 'Getting Started' and 'Basic Techniques' will help you enjoy the sport from the beginning and once you become an enthusiast, constant reference to the chapters on 'Advanced Techniques' and 'Training' will allow you to respond successfully to the challenge of harder and longer courses. Chapter 8 tells you of other attractive alternatives and organising yourself for night orienteering or a two-day

Fig 3   Running fast and effortlessly through mature woodland is an aesthetic experience.

tion situation, whether it is negotiating your local footpaths or exploring wilderness areas on the other side of the world. It will take you into some of our most attractive woodland, forest, heath and moorland, many of which are not normally accessible to the public. In being privileged to go into these areas you should also develop an appreciation for its conservation.

The possibility of getting lost gives the sport an element of adventure. Excitement and nervousness are converted into confidence and joy as each control marker appears before you. When you do get lost, demands are made on self-reliance as you attempt to relocate. The forest can be frightening but it offers a sheltered environment even in the worst weather conditions,

Introduction

mountain marathon becomes almost as exciting as the race itself.

Orienteering is the most enjoyable and fulfilling sport I know. Running fast and effortlessly through mature woodland is an aesthetic experience and finding control points never ceases to lose its magic. I hope that this book will lead you to similar pleasures. Remember, orienteering can be enjoyed all your life.

1 Getting Started

There are orienteering events held on every weekend of the year all over the country. Open events organised by your local club are the best to start with (*see* Useful Addresses). Here you will find courses for the whole range of age and abilities, so, whether you are familiar with maps or not, there will be a course suitable for you. Events usually take place on Sundays, and mid-week evenings from April to September.

PREPARING FOR YOUR FIRST EVENT

Clothing

Orienteers usually wear a light nylon suit with cotton gaiters or 'bramble basher' socks to protect the lower leg, and studded shoes which give a good grip and will not absorb too much water in rough and wet terrain. A T-shirt, light track suit trousers and training shoes are quite adequate to start with. Thought should be given to the weather conditions, extra layers including a waterproof jacket are advisable in winter months and fingerless gloves are a bonus when it is cold. Events are rarely cancelled because of bad weather. Beginners stop a lot to read the map so more clothes are needed to retain body heat and prevent chilling. In warmer weather short sleeves may be worn but shorts are not allowed because of the risk of infection from scratches. An alternative to orienteering shoes with studs is to use orienteering spikes which are preferred by many élite competitors. Remember that

you are likely to get cold and muddy so a change of clothes at the finish is also necessary.

Equipment

It is a good idea to collect all the items in the following list which you will need for a competition and keep them together in a special bag or box.

Fig 4 *A light nylon suit, bramble bashers and studded shoes.*

Polythene bags – to protect the map and control card. Good quality (400 gauge) bags are best for clarity of the map.

Whistle – recommended for safety. Some organisers will not let you start without one. Safety pin it into a pocket.

Compass.

Red ball pens – to copy the course onto your map. Red is the best colour. Felt-tips are too thick and the colour may run in the wet.

Black ball pen – useful for copying control codes.

Safety-pins – at least four are needed to secure the control descriptions and control card.

Wristband – for the control descriptions.

String or five-inch elastic band for the control card.

Insulation tape – to secure your shoe-laces. *Other equipment* – watch, scissors, self-adhesive film, head-band, first-aid, spare laces, insect-repellent are all items which might be needed.

REGISTRATION

When you arrive, ask for help or get an experienced friend to guide you through the initially confusing procedures of registration.

Select a technically easy course if you have only done a little map-reading or a course of medium difficulty if you are familiar with maps and basic navigation techniques. The length of the course can be misleading to athletes. Do not attempt more than three or

Fig 5   The main items of equipment needed to go orienteering.

four kilometres at your first event as even that could take over one hour (*see* Event Standards page 115). A colour-coded Yellow course is the best if you are under eighteen.

Pay your entry fee (£1–£2) and collect a map, control card and control descriptions for the course you have chosen. Competitors start at one-minute intervals so you will be given a start time as well. Allow thirty to fifty minutes from here to get ready and warm up before the start.

PREPARING TO COMPETE

This is most important if you want to run and enjoy your orienteering. Everything should be attached to you except the map. This needs to be given your full attention.

The Map

Check the scale, it will be 1:10,000 or 1:15,000. Mark any 'map corrections' which will be displayed if the map is out of date. Emphasise north with a red pen so that setting the map is easier with a compass. All orienteering maps have magnetic north lines on them so that the magnetic variation does not have to be added as it would have to be on an Ordnance Survey map. Fold the map or cut it so that the competition area is showing but it will go into a small polythene bag to protect it from wet weather and mud.

Control Card

Write in your name on the card and 'stub', then copy the codes from the description list

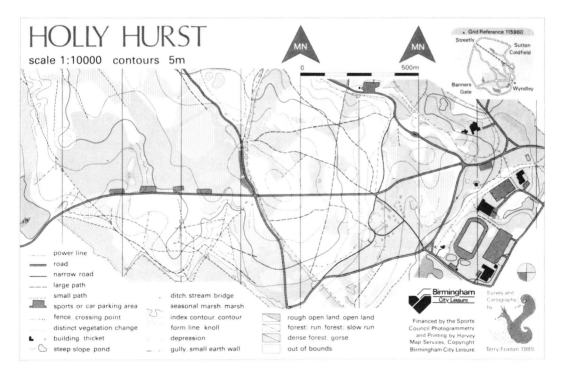

Fig 6   At registration you will be given a map without a course on it.

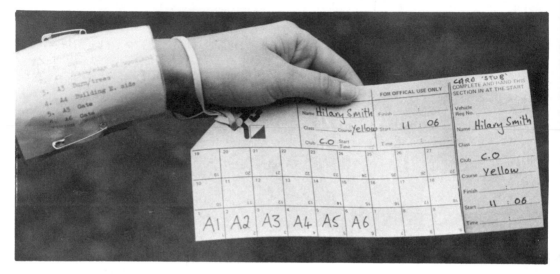

Fig 7   The control card and control descriptions attached to the wrist.

on to the card boxes to give an easy checking system at each control. If it is not of waterproof material, cover the card with transparent film or put it into another polythene bag. Make a hole in the corner (*see* Fig 7) and attach it to your wrist with an elastic band or a piece of cord. Alternatively safety pin it securely to your arm or body making sure that the boxes are free to punch and you can read the codes.

Control Descriptions

These tell you what you are looking for and the code to be found at each control. There will be many controls in the area as well as the ones on your course. Underline every fourth control to make it easier to read while you are running. Cover the list of descriptions with film or put it in another polythene bag and pin over your wrist with two safety-pins; the wristband makes this process easier. Read the descriptions and ask someone if you do not understand any of them.

Almost ready! Pin the whistle inside a pocket for emergencies. Take a red ball pen to copy the controls on to your map. You will need the compass if you have entered a medium to hard course.

Start

Jog up to the start five or ten minutes before your start time. Synchronise your watch, if you wear one, with the start clock. Watch the start system. Find out where you are on the map (ask). Look around to try to get the lie of the land. Finish warming up and stretching. When your time is called or displayed, hand in the 'stub'. This is the organisers' check of who is in the forest. At your start signal run to the master maps which will be close by.

Master Maps

Using a red ball pen copy the control circles on to your map. The centre of each circle shows where the control flag will be, if this is

Fig 8   In a large event the start system organises people into lanes - a
different lane for each colour or class.

Fig 9   Copying from the master maps under a rain shelter.

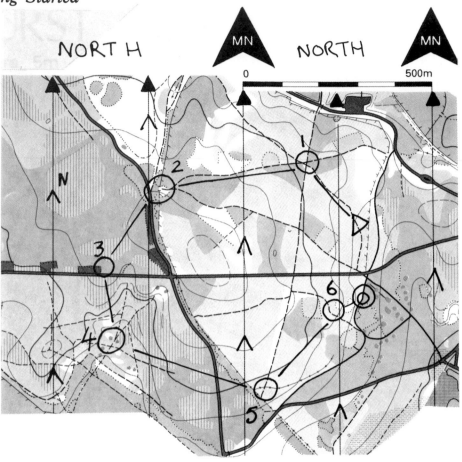

Fig 10   Here is the map after copying the course from the master maps.
Notice that excess map has been cut off or folded under and the
north side has been emphasised. The circles are clear and linked
by lines. The numbers are written outside the circles. No useful
information is covered by these markings.

not clear, read the description. Number the
circles in the correct order, link them with a
line and include the start triangle which is
where the master maps are positioned. The
finish is shown as a double circle. Be careful
that the circles do not obliterate important
information on the map. Although this copying is part of your total time it is worth taking
great care to be accurate, otherwise you
could have the frustration of looking for a
control which is not where you have marked
it.

READY TO GO

Now you can get going. Set your map so
that it lines up with the features around you.
North on the map should now be lying in the
same direction as that shown on the compass. Decide which feature or features you
want to follow to find the first control. Look
for the feature in the area you are in, then set
off to find the first control.

Fig 11   Fold the map and keep your thumb
close to your position. Your thumb
moves as you progress along your
route. Always keep the map set.

Fig 12   The control marker with code number
and pin punches.

Controls

Each control is a three dimensional red and
white triangular marker. It will have an identification code which should correspond with
that on your description list. At every control
there will be a different pin punch with which
to mark your card. Check the code is the
one you want and mark your card in the
correct space for each control.

Finish

Once you have found the last control, there
are usually streamers marking the way to the
finish line. Follow these to the finish and
hand in your card. You must hand in your
card whether you finish the course or not.

Results

Your time is recorded at the finish so that the
time you have taken can be calculated. The
punch marks are checked, your time written
on the stub, and the results are displayed in
time order. A full set of results will be sent if
you leave a self-addressed envelope.

Analysis

How did you get on? Your first goal should
be to find all the controls – this in itself being
an achievement at your first event. When
you have finished a course draw on your
map the route you actually took, including
unintended diversions.

The following list of the basic techniques
which need to be mastered are dealt with in
more detail in the next chapter.

Getting Started

Fig 13 Streamers or tape mark the way to the finish.

Map – know all the map symbols for line features and colours.

Setting the map – always hold the map so the features on the map match the features on the ground.

Thumbing the map – always aim to run with your thumb next to your last known position, this helps to read the map on the move as it is easier to focus on the section of map beside your thumb than on a larger area.

Route choice – learn to use 'handrails' and 'attack points'.

Distance estimation – using the scale of the map, practise estimating distance.

Contours – learn to recognise basic contour features.

Relocation – know what to do when you think you are lost.

Compass – practise setting the map with the compass.

2 Basic Techniques

This section gives you the basic skills for completing a course of easy to medium standard. This would be up to 'Orange' and 'Red' on the British colour-coded system (*see* Event Standards page 117). If you haven't any map-reading background before you start orienteering, then it is advisable to keep with this middle standard for up to twenty events before you progress to the more technical courses. These will slow you down a lot at first, and you will not be able to enjoy running as much.

THE MAP

Orienteering maps are made by orienteers to show the precise shape of the ground, an accurate picture of the path systems, line features, and any other distinct landmarks which can be seen as the orienteer runs through the terrain. The key on the map shows you what all the symbols mean. You will soon become familiar with the most common ones. Maps are normally printed in five colours.

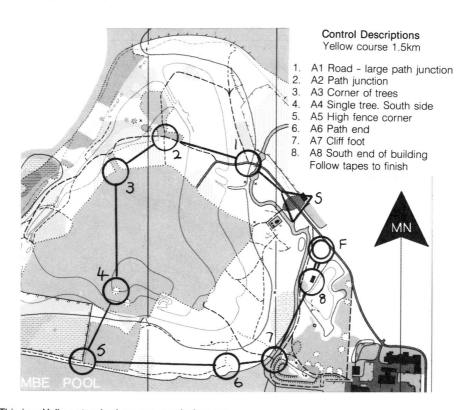

Control Descriptions
Yellow course 1.5km

1. A1 Road - large path junction
2. A2 Path junction
3. A3 Corner of trees
4. A4 Single tree. South side
5. A5 High fence corner
6. A6 Path end
7. A7 Cliff foot
8. A8 South end of building
    Follow tapes to finish

Fig 14   This is a Yellow standard course, graded as easy.

Black symbols

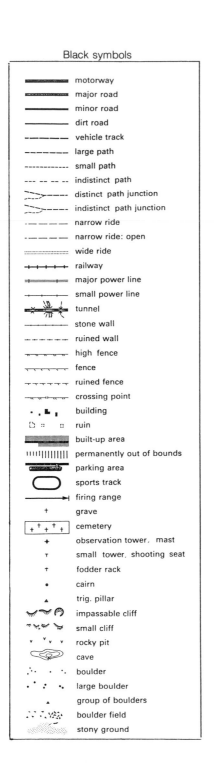

▬▬▬▬▬	motorway
▬▭▬▭▬	major road
———————	minor road
———————	dirt road
– – – – –	vehicle track
- - - - - -	large path
-----------	small path
--- -- -- --	indistinct path
⌐————	distinct path junction
⌐————	indistinct path junction
- — — —	narrow ride
- — — —	narrow ride: open
⋯⋯⋯⋯⋯	wide ride
+++++++	railway
══╪══╪══	major power line
——┬——┬——	small power line
☼	tunnel
———————	stone wall
- - - - - -	ruined wall
⌃⌃⌃⌃⌃⌃	high fence
⌵⌵⌵⌵⌵	fence
⌵ ⌵ ⌵ ⌵	ruined fence
⌵⌵ ⌵⌵ ⌵⌵	crossing point
· ▪ ▪ ▪	building
▫ ▫ ▫	ruin
▬▬▬▬▬	built-up area
‖‖‖‖‖‖‖	permanently out of bounds
▭▭▭	parking area
⬭	sports track
———→	firing range
†	grave
† † † †	cemetery
✦	observation tower, mast
⊤	small tower, shooting seat
⊤	fodder rack
•	cairn
▲	trig. pillar
⌢⌢⌢⌢	impassable cliff
⌢⌢⌢	small cliff
˅ ˅˅ ˅	rocky pit
⬭	cave
⋰ · ⋱	boulder
• ⁚ •	large boulder
▲	group of boulders
⋰⋱ ⋮⋰	boulder field
⣿	stony ground

Blue symbols

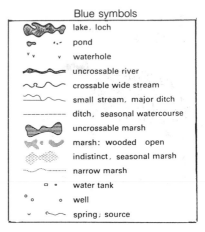

⬮	lake, loch
⬤ ⸱⸰⸱	pond
˅ ˅ ˅	waterhole
⬳	uncrossable river
∿∿	crossable wide stream
∿∿∿	small stream, major ditch
---------	ditch, seasonal watercourse
⬮	uncrossable marsh
≈≈≈	marsh: wooded open
⋯≈⋯	indistinct, seasonal marsh
⋯⌣⋯	narrow marsh
▫ ▪	water tank
° ° °	well
˅ ⌢	spring; source

Brown symbols

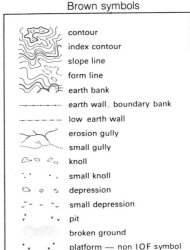

⬭	contour
⬭	index contour
⟋	slope line
⬭	form line
⬭	earth bank
———————	earth wall, boundary bank
- - - - - -	low earth wall
⤳	erosion gully
⋯⋯	small gully
⌒⸱⬤ ⬤⸰	knoll
⸱ · · ⸱⸱	small knoll
⬭ ⬤ ⬤	depression
⌣⌣ ⌣⌣	small depression
˅ ˅ ˅	pit
⸱˅⸱ ·˅	broken ground
⸱ · ⸱˙	platform — non IOF symbol

Yellow vegetation

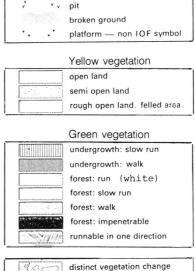

	open land
⸛	semi open land
⸛⸛	rough open land, felled area

Green vegetation

▥	undergrowth: slow run
▦	undergrowth: walk
	forest: run (white)
	forest: slow run
⸛⸛	forest: walk
▬▬	forest: impenetrable
⋰⋱	runnable in one direction

⌐⸱⸱⸱⌐	distinct vegetation change
⸱	indistinct vegetation change

Fig 15 Orienteering Map Symbols.

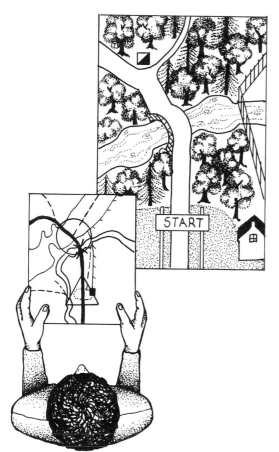

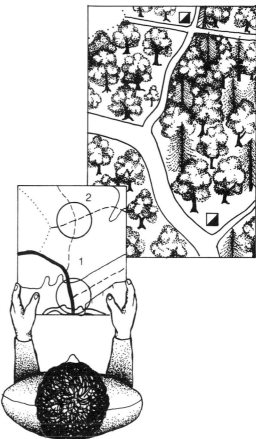

Fig 17   Control 2. Path junction. Do you turn right or left off the road to find number two?

*Fig 16   The map is a symbolised picture of the ground.
Yellow course start: on the road. Control 1. Road and large path junction. The map is set by aligning the road on the map with the road at the start. The building is on your right and the bridge is ahead.*

Map Scale

It is important to know the scale of the map so that you can estimate the distance covered as you follow the features. Measuring more precisely is also useful so that you can judge accurately when you want to leave one specific feature for another.

The most common scales used for orienteering are 1:10,000 and 1:15,000 but often beginners will have a large scale map of

1:5,000. You need to know how far 50 metres and 100 metres are on each map.

1:5,000 – 1mm on the map = 5m on the ground, 1cm = 50m
1:10,000 – 1mm on the map = 10m on the ground, 1cm = 100m
1:15,000 – 1mm on the map = 15m on the ground, 1cm = 150m

Setting and Thumbing the Map

The only way to navigate efficiently and fast is to keep the map 'set' so that the features

Fig 18 *If the map is set correctly it is easy to see which way to turn.*

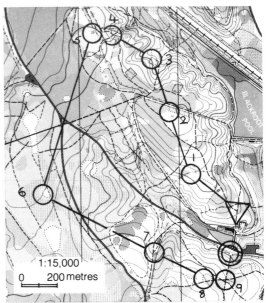

Fig 19 *An Orange course. This course offers a variety of opportunities to make route choices using line features as handrails. It is ideal for practising other important techniques such as aiming off using a compass.*

on the map always match the corresponding features on the ground. For all beginners' courses this can be done without a compass. To help you run and still keep the map set, hold the map, usually in the left hand, with your thumb beside your last known position. If the map is set correctly it is then easy to see whether to run straight or turn left or right.

Route Choice

On easy orienteering courses deciding how to find each control will be very straight-forward. The questions you ask yourself are 'What do I follow?' and 'Which way do I follow it?' Imagine you are navigating round the Yellow course (Fig 14). What would you follow to find each control?

Now look at the map in Fig 14 and for each leg write down which line features link each control and then in which directions you will follow them. As you progress to more technical courses, then choosing a route becomes more interesting. You will often have to select what you consider to be the fastest of several routes. Cutting corners and running straight through the forest are only good options when you can confidently use a compass, judge distance and interpret contour lines. Initially use line features as *handrails* and an *attack point* if the control is isolated.

Handrails

The fastest and safest way to find most of the controls on this course is to follow the line features and use them as handrails – features that you can 'hang on' to.

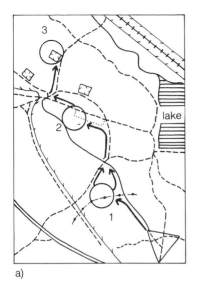

a)

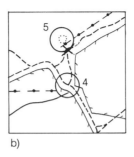

b)

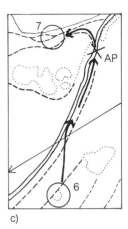

c)

Fig 20 Handrails and attack points.
a) Handrails - the first three controls can be found by using handrails.
b) Leg 4-5 - despite this being a short leg, the clearing will be found most easily if the path junction is used as an attack point. Here you must slow down or stop and navigate carefully into the control.
c) An attack point − the bend in the road − is used on this leg to indicate when to cut across to control 7. If you did not select an attack point it would be easy to miss the opportunity of cutting the corner.

Fig 21 Once you reach the attack point slow right down until you can see where the control is.

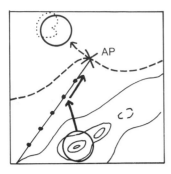

Fig 22   The girl in Fig 21 has used the wall end as her attack point to find the thicket.

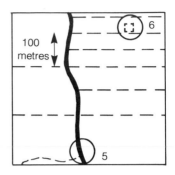

Fig 23   Distance estimation. Pace counting can be useful on easy courses. To find control 6 on the ruin it would be easy to turn along the wrong ride and miss it. Pace count from the bend in the road to be certain of following the ride which leads to the control.

Attack Points

If a control is on an isolated feature such as a clearing, marsh, hill top or ruin, then plan your route to use handrails with an *attack point*. The attack point is a distinct point on a handrail close to the control. It should be easy to find so that you can run as fast as you want to get there. Once you reach the attack point, it is wise to slow right down to a walk until you can see where the control is. This ensures finding the control first time. Estimate the distance from the attack point to the control and, if you are not using a compass, set the map carefully to get the angle right.

Distance Estimation

Many good orienteers develop a feel for how much ground they cover as they run across different types of terrain. This only comes with years of experience and even then this method, which is only guess work, is not very reliable on rough ground or in low visibility.

To be more accurate, the orienteer knows how many double paces he takes to 100 metres. Then, having measured the distance from the map, he makes a quick calculation and counts out the number of double paces he needs.

Calculating Paces

Find a 100 metre stretch of path or track. One way to do this is to measure the distance from the map. Run the distance at least once counting every other pace, i.e. every time either your left or your right foot hits the ground. Keep the stride length as even as possible. Do not run too fast and start again if you lose count. Make a note of the average number of paces you take for 100 metres. Repeat this procedure at walking pace.

A typical running pace on a track would be thirty-eight to forty-eight double paces. A walking pace would be fifty-eight to seventy double paces. Pacing up to 200 metres can be very accurate. Over this distance there is an increasing need to keep map contact and use the compass accurately.

Contours

Contours are shown by brown lines on the map and indicate the shape and steepness of the ground. Understanding contours is the key to good navigation and is essential

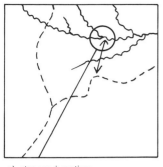

a) stream junction

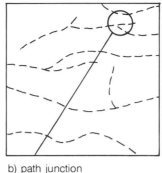

b) path junction

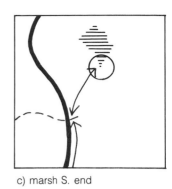

c) marsh S. end

Fig 24   Examples of using pace counting for distance estimation.
a) From the path bend, to be sure of stopping at the right stream.
b) Cutting across several paths and knowing when to stop. Run slowly.
c) From the attack point when there are no other features to lead you to the control. Walk.

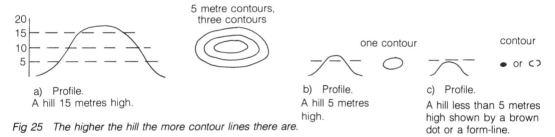

a) Profile.
A hill 15 metres high.

b) Profile.
A hill 5 metres high.

c) Profile.
A hill less than 5 metres high shown by a brown dot or a form-line.

Fig 25   The higher the hill the more contour lines there are.

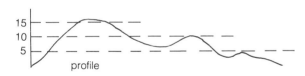

profile

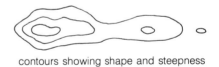

contours showing shape and steepness

Fig 26   The closer the lines the steeper it is. The further apart the flatter it is.
Hilltops are shown by ring contours.

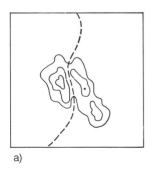

a)

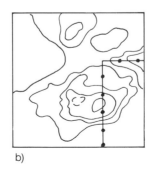

b)

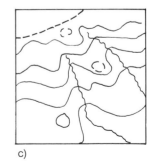

c)

Fig 27   a) The path goes between two hills. Which is higher?
b) The wall goes over the hill and down a valley. Which is the steepest part?
c) The streams are in small valleys or re-entrants. Follow them uphill to find the path. How could you tell which stream you were beside?

Basic Techniques

a landscape picture   contours

Fig 28 Re-entrants. a is a small shallow re-entrant shown by one contour. b
        is a large re-entrant with a bend in it. c is narrow with steep sides. d
        is broad and softer. e splits into two re-entrants going in two
        directions.

Fig 29 Follow the path through this contour
        pattern and try to visualise when you
        would go up or down a re-entrant.

if you are going to become a successful
orienteer. The best way to learn about
contours is to go out with a map and look at
the ground, comparing it with the contour
lines shown on the map. Every bend and
squiggle on the map means something.

A contour line joins points of equal height,
and most orienteering maps show contours
at 5 metre intervals. Look at the contour
patterns and hill profiles (see Figs 25–7).
When you look at a contour pattern on a
map you should try and picture what the
ground will look like – how high? how steep?
what shapes?

Re-entrants and spurs occur frequently in
orienteering and there is sometimes confu-
sion in knowing exactly what they look like.
A re-entrant is a small valley. If you stand in
a re-entrant the ground on both sides and in

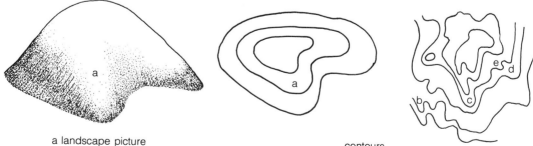

a landscape picture   contours

Fig 30 Spurs. The contours show a, b, c and d as distinct spurs with two
        or more contour lines. e is also a spur shown by a single contour
        line. Where are the spurs in Fig 31?

Fig 31 Form-lines. Look carefully. This area shows many form-lines which improve the map picture for the orienteer.

front of you rises. A spur is the opposite to a re-entrant. It is like a nose of ground pointing downhill. A spur may be shown by one or more contour lines.

In very detailed areas extra information which will improve the picture for the orienteer is shown by form-lines. These are broken brown lines which would not be shown by the regular contour interval. In

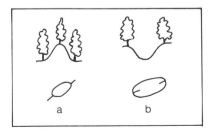

Fig 32 'Tags' are sometimes shown on the downhill side of the contour. a shows a small hill or knoll. b shows a hollow or depression.

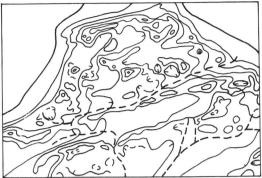

Fig 33 This area of sand-dunes shows form-lines and 'tags' to give an improved picture of the ground.

undulating areas where it is difficult to interpret which are the hills and which are the valleys, small 'tags' are added to the downhill side of the contour.

RELOCATION

Relocation is finding out where you are when you are lost.

Most orienteers get lost at every event they go to. They do not always know exactly where they are all the time, and frequently cannot find control points because they are running too fast and losing their place on the map. This is part of the challenge of the sport – the balance of your speed with the certainty of knowing where you are. How fast can you go yet still read the map and find control points? It is easy to get this wrong, get lost, panic and finish up running round in circles wasting even more time. Do not worry, this is a common occurrence with all orienteers. A strategy for relocation is essential.

As soon as you are not certain where you are, slow down and try to pick up features you see on the map. If you are still lost do not

Fig 34   As soon as you are not certain where
you are, slow down and try to pick up
features you see on the map.

panic! Try to think coolly. Do not keep
wandering about. Stop where there are at
least two distinctive features which you
would expect to find on the map. Set the
map to north and try to match the pattern of
features with those on the map. With the
features you see, you can really only be in
one place.

If you still cannot place yourself, think
carefully and recall the features you followed
from the last control or your last known
position. Could you have left the control
180° in the wrong direction? If after only one
or two minutes you are still lost you should
make your way to a major line feature. Find
out exactly where you are on the map and
then continue navigating to the control. If, at
this stage you are worried or not enjoying
the experience for any reason then you can

make your way to the finish! Ask someone
the way back if necessary.

If you become so lost that you have no
idea what to do, and you cannot find
someone to ask, then you can use the
emergency signal on your whistle. This is six
long blasts repeated after a long pause (half
a minute). If you hear the rescue reply of
three short blasts then respond with your six
again so that you can be found.

Do not forget to report to the finish even if
you have had to retire. This is one of the
rules, so that a check can be made that
everyone has returned.

BASIC
COMPASS TECHNIQUES

When you start orienteering on the easy
courses such as White and Yellow in the
British colour-coded system, a compass
should not be necessary. As soon as you
start to progress from following simple line
features, though, a compass becomes an
essential part of the orienteer's equipment.

Compasses

Choosing the right compass is difficult
before you have learned how to use one.
However, for versatility, measurement of
distance and accuracy, the protractor
compass with an exchangeable map scale
is recommended. If you find that you do not
use the compass because you prefer map-
reading then a thumb compass will help to
keep the map set correctly and save you a
lot of time.

Use some cord to attach the compass to
your wrist, so that it is easy to hold in your
hand, even if you drop it, yet is not so tight
that you cannot turn it round on the map. Do
not wear it round your neck.

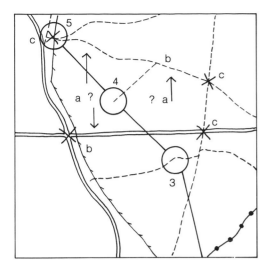

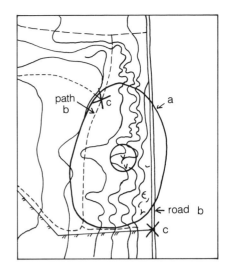

Fig 35   Relocation. If you are lost do not waste time wandering about.
   a) Identify the area of the map you know you are in.
   b) Look for the nearest distinct line feature.
   c) Using your compass head out for this as quickly as possible.
   d) Locate yourself precisely on this line feature (X).
   e) Continue navigating carefully to the control.

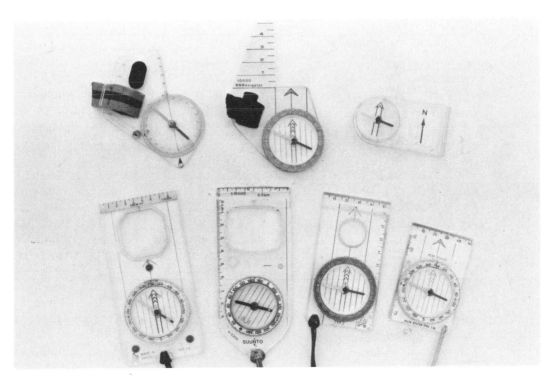

Fig 36   A selection of compasses used by orienteers. The bottom row
   shows the protractor type of compasses.

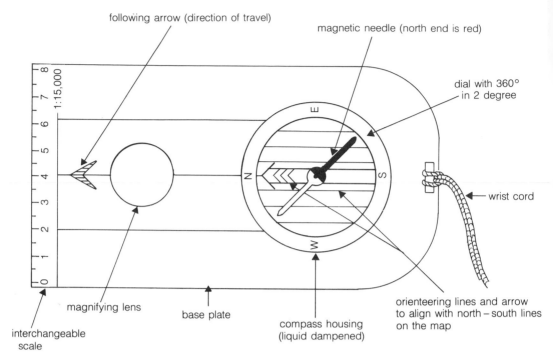

following arrow (direction of travel)

magnetic needle (north end is red)

1:15,000

dial with 360°
in 2 degree

wrist cord

magnifying lens

base plate

compass housing
(liquid dampened)

orienteering lines and arrow
to align with north – south lines
on the map

interchangeable
scale

Fig 37   Parts of a protractor compass.

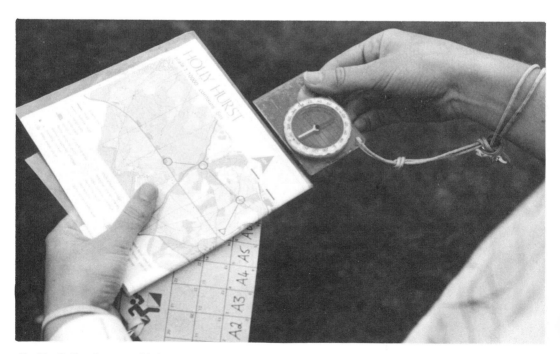

Fig 38   Setting the map, Method 1.

Look after your compass. Make sure it is kept clean – pieces of grit can easily jam the housing – and store it away from metal objects which may affect the magnetic needle. Replacement parts can be obtained from most stockists.

Setting the Map With a Compass

Orienteering maps always have magnetic north lines marked on them. When these are parallel to the magnetic needle in the compass then you know the map is accurately set or orientated.

When you are only using the compass for setting the map it is best to keep 'N' on the dial in line with the following arrow.

Method 1 – compass held in the opposite hand to the map: hold the map with your thumb where you are, looking along the map feature or the line you want to follow. Identify the north–south lines on the map. Hold the compass flat, close to the map and let the needle settle. The red end points to north.

Turn yourself with the map until the red needle is pointing the same way as the north lines on the map. If you are still holding the map correctly, the feature on the map you want to follow should now be in front of you. The map is now set.

This method can also be used for relocation. It is necessary to practise until you completely understand this method of setting the map.

Method 2 – compass held in the same or opposite hand as the map: put the compass on the map with the long edge of the base plate lying parallel with the feature you want

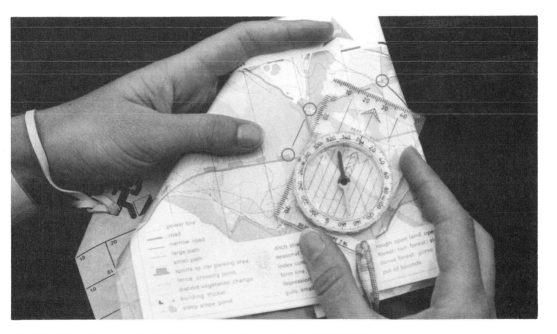

Fig 39   Setting the map, Method 2: the magnetic needle lies parallel with the north-south lines on the map.

Basic Techniques

to follow. The 'following arrow' on the base plate should point in the direction you want to go along that feature.

Turn yourself with map and compass together until the magnetic needle lies parallel with the north–south lines on the map. There is no need to turn the dial, just look at the needle. The map is now set to north, and you should be facing along the feature you want to follow.

If you find it comfortable you can run with a protractor compass on the map all the time. This is similar to using a thumb compass. You can check constantly that the map is set

Fig 40 You run with a thumb compass on the map all the time. Keep the needle to map north all the time.

but 'thumbing' the map becomes more difficult. It is your choice whether you hold the compass in the same hand or the opposite hand to the map.

Method 2 using a protractor compass leads easily into the next step which is taking a compass bearing.

Taking a Compass Bearing from the Map

A more accurate way of finding the direction of the way you want to go is to take a bearing from the map. This is measuring the angle between north (0°) and the route line you want to follow.

Put the compass edge parallel to the feature you want to follow or parallel to whatever line of travel you want to take. Turn the dial until north ('N') on the dial points to map north and the red lines in the compass housing are parallel to the N/S lines on the map. Hold the compass flat and straight in front of you. Turn your body with the map and compass together until the needle lies along the north–south line in the housing.

What you have done is to use the compass as a protractor measuring the angle of the direction in which you want to travel using north as 0°. Knowing magnetic north is zero it is then possible to pinpoint any direction by measuring the angle. Now you are all set for cutting corners and running across country to navigate from one control to another. The compass is essential for fast and efficient orienteering, but it must always be used as a back-up to your map-reading. The controls are found by reading the map. The compass helps you select and keep to your chosen route.

Always take an accurate bearing even if you only use the direction as a rough guide.

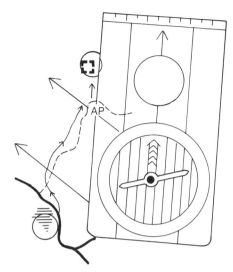

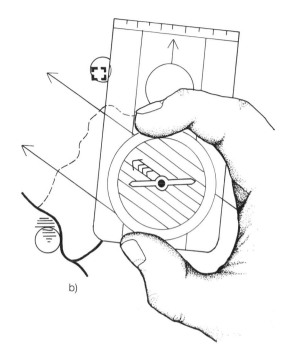

a) attack point - the path bend,
to the control - the ruin

b)

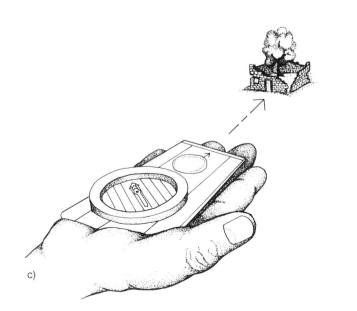

c)

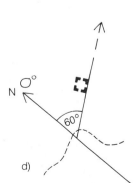

d)

Fig 41 Taking a compass bearing from the map.

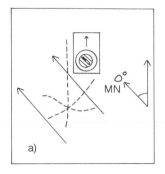 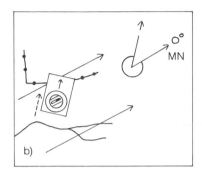 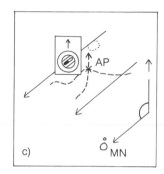

Fig 42 Three ways of using a compass bearing.
a) Checking the direction of a line feature.
b) Cutting corners and aiming off.
c) Finding a control feature from an attack point.

Fig 43 The compass is essential for fast and efficient orienteering.

Aiming Off

If a control or attack point is on a line feature it is faster and safer to aim deliberately to one side, so that if you come to the line feature and cannot see the control marker you know which way to turn to locate it. It is one of the best techniques in any sort of navigation.

Attack Points

If the control is on a small feature and your route is planned to an attack point, use a compass bearing to lead you accurately into the control from the attack point.

Other ways of using the compass and aiming off will be found in Chapter 3.

Safety Bearings

A safety bearing is a cardinal direction (north, south, east or west) which can be easily followed, to lead the lost orienteer to a major road or boundary which leads back to the finish area. In some events a safety bearing will be included on the control description list, in others you will have to work it out

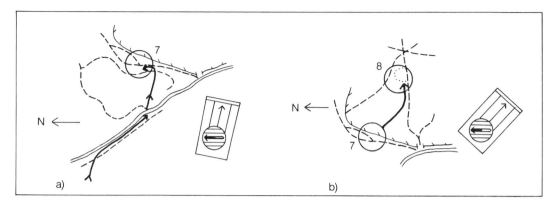

Fig 44 Aiming off. a) To find control 7 on the orange course (Fig 19). Run along the road until it bends. Take a compass bearing to the path to the right of the control site (path junction). Follow the bearing. When you come to the second path turn left and run along the path until you see the junction and the control marker.
b) Control 8 is clearing N.W. edge. One route choice is to aim off to the path, then run along the path to the clearing. This could be the fastest route on this leg. The alternative is to follow the paths as handrails.

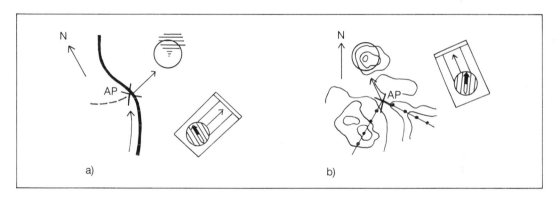

Fig 45 Accurate compass bearing from an attack point. Use with pace counting and map reading to find the control first time.

for yourself. As long as you have a compass then it is usually a simple matter to follow one of these four directions.

If the forest is thick and you prefer to keep to the tracks and paths, try and follow these as close as possible to the direction in which you want to go. Ask someone to help you if you are really lost, or use the whistle.

RULES

Here is a selection of the most relevant rules which apply to anyone starting orienteering.

1. Disqualification will occur if:
   a) Controls are visited out of order.
   b) One or more controls are missed completely.
   c) Incorrect controls have been visited, shown by the punch patterns.

Fig 46 'Orienteers should be independent unless entered as a pair or group.'
Following is not allowed.

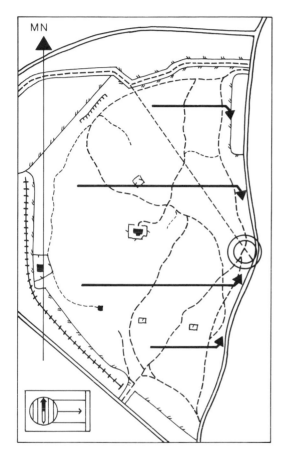

Fig 47 Safety bearings. In this area the lost
orienteer should head east to find the
road from which the finish can be
easily found.

d) Out of bounds areas have been crossed, or walls and fences, when there are compulsory crossing points. Gardens and fields with crops are always out of bounds.

e) Any competitor is seen deliberately following or seeking information from other competitors. Orienteers should be independent unless entered as a pair or a group.

2. Always report to the finish whether you have completed the course or not, otherwise someone will search for you.

3. Body and full leg cover must be worn. Short-sleeved tops are allowed, but not shorts.

4. Carry a compass in unknown terrain and understand the use of a safety bearing.

5. A whistle should be carried in case of emergency.

6. A watch is recommended for course closure times.

7. The Country Code must always be respected: no litter, no fires, close gates, use crossing points on walls and fences.

3 Advanced Techniques

Mastering the basic techniques can take over a year for many beginners whilst others, usually those with some previous map-reading experience, can pick them up in a matter of days.

As soon as you are running fast round an Orange or Red course it is time to pursue the finer techniques of the sport. At this advanced level you will experience a new dimension. Running strongly through trackless, forested terrain and being in complete contact with the map is a joy to experience. It is said that it takes seven to ten years to make a top orienteer.

READING THE MAP ON THE RUN

This is not easy but can be learned with practice. First of all, it is essential to keep your thumb on the map all the time. As you progress along each leg so your thumb moves along the map so that when you glance at it you focus on the area just beside your thumb. Keep the map folded so that you only have to focus on a small area. Running through rough terrain and even running along a track takes up quite a lot of attention and concentration, so that if you look at the map for more than two or three seconds you are likely to trip over something or somebody! Run with your map in front of you, not swinging it backwards and forwards as if you were running on an athletics track. Glance at the map several times to get the information you want. Each glance will give you more of the picture that

you need. Gradually absorb more information, first picking out the area you want, then the major features along the route, then the detail. It will be necessary to walk or stop to read any intricate detail.

You should be able to take compass bearings and measure distance as you are running along. Practise reading a map on the run round the streets at night, using the street lights to absorb information. You will quickly improve.

Most time is saved by choosing the best route and following it fluently by applying the right technique at the right time. This is where these advanced techniques can help you.

MAP CONTACT

Maintaining contact with the map is not just reading all the information along the chosen route. It is selecting what you require, so that you can run as fast as you want yet still know where you are.

You will also need to slow down, walk or even stop to read the map. Learn to select the most relevant detail required to execute each part of your route. Then you will reduce the time you have to look at the map, cutting out hesitations, as well as developing a better rhythm of running and looking.

'Easy' Courses and Legs

Controls linked by line features make map contact and running straightforward. As you follow each feature you need to know:

Fig 48 Run with your map in front of you.

Advanced Techniques

Fig 49   It will be necessary to walk or stop to read the detail from the map.

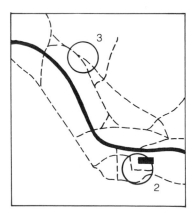

Fig 50   An easy leg which will require concentration to follow the path system. Keep looking at the map and check off every junction.

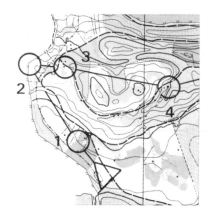

Fig 51   This 'easy' course will require good map contact to know when to turn off for controls 1, 2, and 3 and a good feeling for distance to know when to look out for the boulder controls at 3 and 4. The markers will be in sight of the track.

a) where you are along that feature; b) when you need to leave it, and c) what feature you will follow next. Concentrate on orienteering, not just running, even if you have a long track run ahead of you. Keep looking at the map, picking out junctions or large features, and anticipate seeing them as you progress. These will ensure that you maintain contact. If you are finding this easy, use the opportunity to look ahead at the route choices for the rest of the course. Remember to keep running, keep your thumb moving along the route and gather the information you need in a series of short glances. If you stop looking at the map completely, you will find that your thoughts can drift away from the orienteering. This is when mistakes are made and you will lose your racing rhythm. Beginners can try pace counting on these easy legs. Pacing is also invaluable for knowing when to look out for small paths and rides which are easy to miss.

'Medium' Courses and Legs

Map contact is essential if you want to find the controls easily. To keep up your speed it is necessary to simplify the information taken from the map. First of all look for the line features which you can follow. These should stand out in your mental picture whilst all the other map detail can go out of focus. As you follow these line features you monitor your progress by bringing the detail on the map just ahead of you back into focus. It is the same when you start cutting corners and leaving handrails. Pick out the line and large features which you will cross, ignoring everything else. Now you can mentally tick these off as you cross them until you reach the feature you want. Pace counting (*see* below) will help as well to confirm that you are crossing, for instance, the path or stream on the map, and not an unsurveyed sheep track or ditch.

Medium difficult courses often have controls placed on large features such as clearings, marshes and hill tops. Use an attack point or aim off and give your full attention to everything on the map in this part of your route. Look out in the terrain for each feature in turn and use as many as you need to lead you to the control. This increase in map contact forces you to slow down. Make yourself do this if you want to find the controls first time.

'Hard' Courses and Legs

The quality of a good hard course is measured by the number of legs demanding continuous map reading. The longer the leg the harder it becomes. If there are no line features to 'collect' along the route, the orienteer must navigate, reading contours and using any other information he can from the map.

Fig 52 A medium difficult leg. Route choice is influenced by the line features you can follow. The ditches, streams and paths should stand out when you first look for a route. Your four main areas of map contact are shown on the map. Follow the line features, linking them up by taking a compass bearing to help you to run in the right direction. In between the four areas keep glancing at the map to reassure yourself that you are following the right line. Aim off to the track in area four, slow down and use the ditch-track junction as your attack point. The contours showing the shape of the ground will also help you to keep map contact in the first half of the leg.

The principles of keeping map contact are the same as on the easier courses. Instead of using line features to check progress, distinctive shaped hills, ridges, deep valleys,

Advanced Techniques

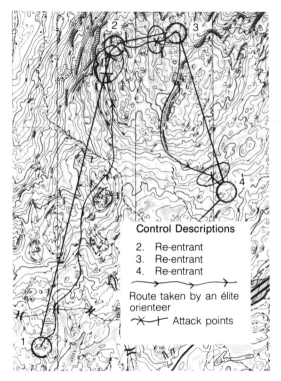

Control Descriptions

2. Re-entrant
3. Re-entrant
4. Re-entrant

Route taken by an élite orienteer

✕―† Attack points

Fig 53 Part of a 'hard' course in open fell terrain. Route choice is critical for map contact and optimum speed. Legs 1-2 and 3-4 would involve more climbing if the straight line option was taken. All the controls need to be attacked accurately because of the risk of parallel errors. On leg 2-3 the stream half-way along is a useful collecting feature but you must know exactly where you cross it to attack control 3 cleanly. Lines of valleys and cliffs and a single contour were used as handrails. The continuous contact approach proved successful.

lines of crags or distinct vegetation changes are selected and ticked off as the orienteer progresses through a corridor of terrain. As the control is approached the map is studied in greater detail. A clear mental picture is created and the athlete navigates carefully to find the control.

Route choice is critical if you are to make map contact easier for yourself. The skilful use of the compass and the use of distance estimation are also important.

'Hard' courses will be Green, Blue and Brown at colour-coded events, and 'A' class courses at Badge Events and National Events (*see* Event Standards page 115). The degree of hardness or technical demands of a course will also depend on the area being used. The standard will vary according to which part of the country you are in. It is difficult to make a course technically demanding if the area is full of paths and other linear features.

When you first enter these harder courses it is recommended that you try to keep continuous map contact and lose some running speed. This style of orienteering (*see* page 54) is used by many world class orienteers all the time. It is also the best approach to use in British open moorland and fell areas.

Large and distinct features are selected

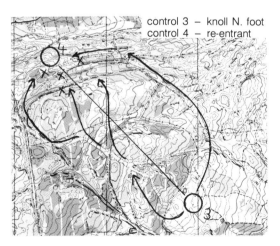

control 3 – knoll N. foot
control 4 – re-entrant

Fig 54 A hard leg designed to test route choice in steep woodland terrain with mixed vegetation. Do you choose the straight corridor using rides, attacking from the line of crags to the south or the longer but safer route following the old wall to the north?

from the map, and a compass bearing gives you the line to follow between them. The routine continues with two procedures. Firstly, look at the map, form pictures of the main features 100–200 metres in front of you, and locate them in the terrain as you follow your compass bearing. This is called *map memory*. Meanwhile, watch out for other features and glance at your map to try to identify them. This is called *terrain memory*.

These two simultaneous procedures will confirm that you are not only where you think you are, but also where you want to be! The first part is relating map to ground, backed up by the second part which is relating ground to map. The compass gives you the direction to follow, but pace counting as well allows you to keep running between major features when you cannot make the map and ground match.

Interpretation of Contour Detail

Immediate and accurate interpretation of the contours and visualising the ground from a quick glance at the map is the art of the skilful orienteer. The best way to learn about reading contours is to go into an area with lots of contour detail on a good map. First of all, plot a line which weaves its way across and around the distinctive contour features, then follow this line slowly through the terrain. Visualise where the line is going, then look at the terrain and make the picture real. Do this for 50–100 metres at a time.

When planning and following a route with only contours to help you, try hard to keep map contact. It is important to simplify the picture as much as possible. Remember that it is the contour lines which show you how much climbing will be involved on any route. The orienteer must look for this and consider

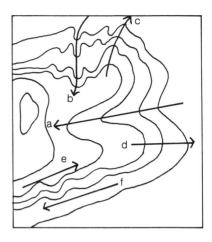

Fig 55   These arrows show how contour features can be used as handrails. a and b are long re-entrants, c and d are spurs, e and f changes of gradient.

it against other less strenuous and possibly faster choices. Many contour features can be used as handrails for route choice. A long re-entrant, a ridge, a change in gradient or a single contour line can be seen on the map and followed quickly and safely.

You will find that every bend in a contour line will show a change of shape in the

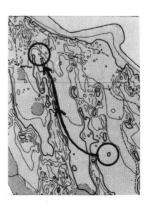

Fig 56   These sand-dune ridges can be used as very clear handrails to follow. Run along the flat ground keeping the slope to one side.

Advanced Techniques

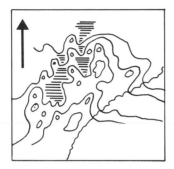

Fig 57 *You are standing on a knoll at the end of a spur. By setting the map with the compass and matching the relationship of spurs, knolls and re-entrants you should be able to locate. Is the spur pointing north, north-west or north-east? Does it have a marsh or a stream on one or both sides? How steep is it at the end of the spur (two or more contours close together)? What shape and direction are the re-entrants on either side? Select a knoll and ask someone else to guess which one it is as you describe its situation.*

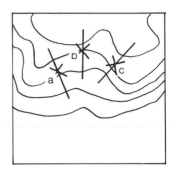

Fig 58 *It should be straightforward to identify your position on this hillside by setting the map accurately with the compass and matching the angle of slope.*

ground which can be used to help you navigate. Setting the map with the compass will help you see how the relationship of one contour feature to another should appear on the ground. It is these patterns of contour features which will help you relocate. The compass can be used to check the direction of long contour features and also the angles of slopes.

ADVANCED DISTANCE ESTIMATION

After thirty to fifty events you will be beginning to get a better feel for the distance you cover using different scales of map. However, there are many situations where relying only on feel and the map will leave you hesitant and very often lost. If you can get into the habit of counting paces so that it

becomes second nature, then you do not have to think too much about it. Pacing accurately means you can run faster without having to keep such close contact with the map in the early part of a leg. It is easy to count however fast you run, but you can only read the map at below maximum pace. Linked with a compass bearing and map contact every 200–400 metres this becomes a very fast fluent method of orienteering.

Pace Counting

There are four ways of measuring and counting paces. Always count double paces.

1. Measure the distance, calculate the total paces then count as you run. This is the best method for distances under 300 metres where error should be minimal.
2. Measure the distance, then count in hundreds of metres, e.g. 350 metres at 50 double paces per hundred. Count 50, 50, 50 then 25. This way it is easy to add or subtract a few paces for each hundred metres according to the nature of the terrain. Care must be taken to remember how much distance has been covered.

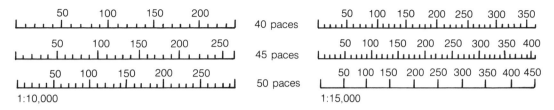

Fig 59   These are pacing scales which can be made and taped to the end of your compass. You will need a different pace scale for each scale of map.

3.   Measure directly into paces, using a pacing scale instead of a scale measuring metres. This method does save some calculations initially and is useful if your pace does not vary over different types of terrain. Extra paces can easily be added in rough or steep terrain or taken off for easy tracks and downhill. The disadvantage of this system is in relocating if you are unable to make map contact when you come to the end of your paces. It is easier to work back on to the map with distance rather than paces, e.g. 'I know I must have come at least 250 metres so I must be in this area of the map'.

4.   Another way of using pace counting is to count by distance off the map. Count paces to a distinct feature (a) then seeing that the next measurable distance is about

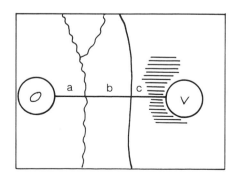

Fig 60   Pace counting by distance off the map. Distance a is the same as b. c is half a or b.

the same, count the same number again (b). Distance c is about half a and b so count half the paces counted from a to b.

Keep an open mind, try all the methods and select the one that works best for you.

The Use of Pace Counting

You should have three figures you can recall for pace counting, depending on the terrain and the general situation. Each of these is an average for 100 metres:

1.   A track or path running pace, e.g. 45 double paces.
2.   A terrain running pace, e.g. 50 double paces.
3.   A walking pace, e.g. 60 double paces.

These are typical examples provided by the author. It is exceedingly difficult to estimate the exact number of paces each individual will need, due to the variation in types of terrain and fitness. Therefore, pace counting should only be used as a back-up system to your map-reading and use of the compass. Do not expect to be within less than five double paces of your estimated figure over 100 metres. This means that the further you count the greater the possible error. It is these variations which contribute to people giving up pacing because they say it

Advanced Techniques

Fig 61   The author: 'I keep continuous map contact. I pace count and use my compass all the time.'

very steep slope

index contours only shown

1:15,000

Fig 62   The use of pace counting. 'I started counting paces as I left the control to make sure I knew when to look for the small path. The terrain was very rough. I ran round the track and counted again from the track junction. The steep slope was covered in bracken, after 150 metres (70 paces) I saw a break and headed up the hill. I measured the distance and took a bearing to the bank end, my attack point. I pace counted because it could be hidden by the bracken. Finally I measured and counted again on a bearing as I continued climbing. I went slowly as I didn't want to miss the marker. I allowed extra paces for the rough ground and the hillside and stopped just above the control in the re-entrant.'

doesn't work. If you think positively you will appreciate the value of knowing when to slow down, because you should have paced the distance and then you can look out for the feature you want to find. You will find that pace counting saves you a lot of time. It gives you confidence to run faster and reduces the map checking stops.

Pace counting is useful during the first part of each leg. In this 'rough' orienteering phase, use it to help you check-off major features and to know when to turn off line features. It is of greatest value in attacking the control when it is combined with map contact and a compass bearing. This is where a reliable walking pace is invaluable to avoid overshooting.

Use the scale on the compass to measure the distance to the nearest 10 metres. Be as accurate as possible, otherwise the possibility of error will increase if the distance is measured incorrectly. On a map with a scale of 1:10,000 it is easy to measure distance accurately where 1mm represents 10 metres.

Finally remember the map has usually been made by an orienteer who is not a professional cartographer so it can sometimes give a confusing representation of the ground. Pacing allows you to ignore the map on these occasions and continue confidently on a compass bearing.

COMPASS

The compass is the orienteer's main piece of navigational equipment apart from the map. Learning how to use it efficiently will help you to orienteer more smoothly and make fewer mistakes.

Taking and Following a Bearing on the Run

This is best done in stages so that you can also watch where you are putting your feet. First place the compass on the map with the edge, or a parallel line, along the route you want to take. Then 'dial north', and re-check the edge. Be precise.

The needle must be allowed to settle if you want to follow the bearing accurately. This means that you must slow down and walk, holding the compass flat and in front of you. Then pick out a distinctive tree or feature as far ahead as possible along your sighting line. Now run. The further away this point is, the more accurately you will follow the bearing.

Small errors in placing the compass, the bearing, the map and aligning the needle can add up to a minimum of 5° from the line you want to follow. If you look at your compass the swinging of the needle can add another 10° to this variation.

When you use your compass you should decide whether you need to follow it accurately which is *precision* or *fine* compass, or use it just to give you a general direction; this is *rough* compass.

Fine compass is normally used from an

Fig 63   Hold the compass flat and in front of you.

attack point to the control, especially when there is little map detail to guide you in. Rough compass is used to cut through blocks of terrain, aiming off, and running out of a control.

Running on the Needle

This is rough compass without taking a bearing at all. Most thumb compasses are used on this principle. The following arrow gives you your line of travel as usual, but you run at an angle to the magnetic needle instead of dialling a bearing.

By looking at the map you decide in which direction you want to go. If it is north or south you follow the red or white end of the needle, if east or west you run at right angles to the needle.

If, like some orienteers, you prefer to run

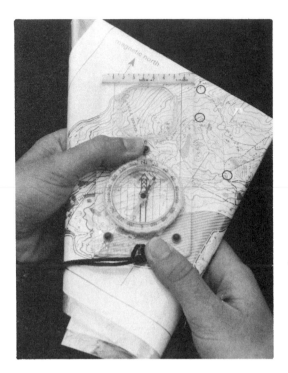

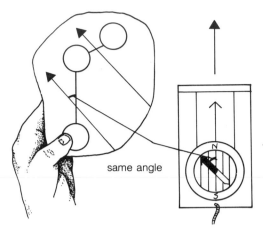

same angle

Fig 65 *Running on the needle. Holding the map, looking along the direction you want to go (N.W), observe where the north-south lines are on the map and run with the magnetic needle parallel to these lines. The housing is dialled to north to assist in keeping the needle at the right angle.*

Fig 64 *Running on the needle. With the compass on or off the map, you run at an angle formed by the magnetic needle and the direction in which you want to go. In this case about 30° west of north.*

with the compass on the map in the same hand, then running on the needle is basically a matter of keeping the needle parallel with the north–south lines. You are running, making sure the map is kept set with the compass (*see* Method 2, pages 31-2).

The compass can also be used to check the direction of line features and slopes and increase your confidence in knowing that you are running in the right direction. The scales on the base plate measure distance, and the magnifying glass can be used for clarifying map detail.

The compass is an invaluable aid, but you must put all these points into practice in order to increase your enjoyment and skill in the use of it.

ROUTE CHOICE

One of the most attractive aspects of orienteering is that the choice of route is yours. Using the information on the map, and knowing your own strengths and weaknesses, it is up to you how you find your way between each control. It is worth learning the skills and strategies described here to enable you to follow your chosen route efficiently and fast.

Factors Affecting Your Choice of Route

Route Planning

Always plan your route backwards, that is select a distinct attack point within 150 metres of the control, then plan your route to the attack point. This often puts a different perspective on the choice of route. You should do this planning during the previous leg so that you do not have to stop once you

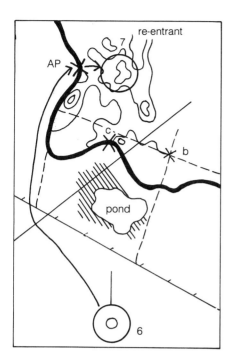

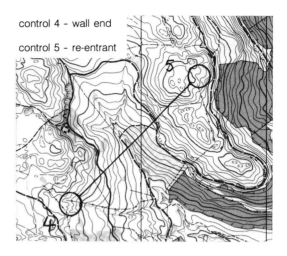

control 4 - wall end

control 5 - re-entrant

*Fig 67   Straight or round. The road and ride
route to the left is 300 metres longer
than the straight route which goes
across the valley. The straight route
involves twice as much climbing (80
metres). Which way would you go?
The routes are quite even, you must
make your decision quickly.*

*Fig 66   Plan the route backwards. The best
attack point for this control is the road
bend (AP). This influences the route
choice. The other routes would attack
the control from the ride junction (b)
or the road bend (c).*

have punched at the control. Controls are
more easily found if your route can include
distinct features which will lead you in to
them. In this situation you devise an attacking line or corridor instead of an attack point.

Some routes are safe, others risky. You
will reduce the risk of straight line options if
you learn which map features will be
obvious in the terrain and how to use the
ground in the vicinity of the control to
simplify finding the marker.

Straight or Round

The choice of going straight or using a
longer path route is a typical orienteering
problem. You have to weigh up the options

and make a decision within a few seconds.

A useful guide in making one of these
route choice decisions is to look at how far
away the track or path is from the straight
line at its widest point. This will be approx-
imately the extra distance you will have to
run if you go round. If you know you can run
20 per cent further on a road in the same
time as going straight through the terrain,
then you are beginning to accumulate information to help you choose your route.

The other attractions of choosing a road
route are that it gives your legs and mind a
rest from running through the terrain, it
allows you to look at the next leg and even
the rest of the course, and make what could
be critical route choice decisions, and it
takes away some of the stress which can
accumulate when concentrating hard on
keeping map contact on straight line routes.

These route choices are not always
straightforward. Other factors which need to

Advanced Techniques

Fig 68 *Route choice - tracks and paths are an attractive option when there is a choice of straight or round.*

be considered include the amount of climbing involved (running up is easier on a track but there is little difference coming down), the type of terrain and how easy it is to run through it, the amount of precise navigation needed along the route and your experience and skill in reading the map.

Making the Control 'Bigger'

Small point features such as a depression, a boulder, or a knoll can be hard to find. Wherever possible you should look for features around the control site to make it 'longer' or 'bigger'. This is linked with aiming

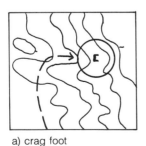
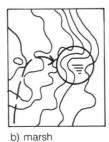
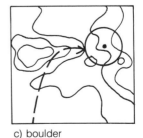

a) crag foot   b) marsh   c) boulder

Fig 69 *Make the control bigger. a) Aim off to the distinct spur which leads to the crag. The spur makes the control easier to find. b) The re-entrant makes the control longer and aiming off is used again. c) The boulder is a small feature but the distinct ridge above it makes it longer.*

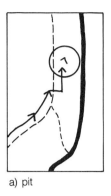 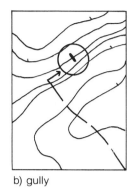 

a) pit   b) gully   c) re-entrant

Fig 70   Aiming off to simplify the control.
a) Pace count in from the path the same distance as the pit. Turn
and run parallel with the path to find the control.
b) A small feature on a slope with only the top of the hill as an
attack point. Aim off, pace count from the top of the hill and also
look out for the steepening in the slope. Turn along the slope.
c) Aim off to run along the top of the slope. Pace count from the
path junction.

off to attack the control. Try to approach controls from above as you have a wider vision looking down than when you are looking up a hill. Aiming off can be used again to make a small feature easy to find.

ROUTE EXECUTION – THE DEVELOPMENT OF STYLE

Having planned your route the real test comes in executing it – running and putting together all the techniques to find the controls as quickly and as efficiently as possible. For successful orienteering you should develop a strategy or system which works best for you. Route execution will involve the following sequence repeated for each leg and control:

1. Running as fast as possible to the control area, keeping map contact only as much as you need to locate in the area of the control.

2. Selecting an attack point or large feature within 150 metres of the control.
3. Navigating carefully and accurately into the control.
4. Punching at the control and passing through it as quickly as possible.

Most mistakes are caused by the orienteer not following this sequence at one point or more. The orienteer usually runs too fast or does not maintain enough map contact in the area of control. Here is the challenge of orienteering – balancing your speed with the certainty of knowing where you are.

Orienteering Styles

Balancing speed with map contact can be done in several ways. The way you choose should be the one which gives you most pleasure as well as success. The style you develop should maximise your strengths and take account of your weaknesses.

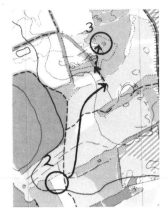

a) flat terrain

······································▶ red

– – – – – – – ▶ amber

―――――――▶ green

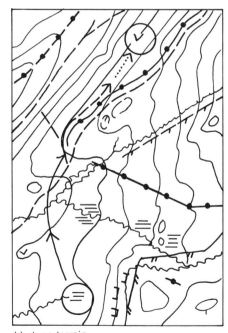

b) steep terrain

Fig 71 Traffic-light orienteering in two different types of terrain. The 'green' section is fast with rough orienteering, then 'amber' with increased concentration to find the attack point. The 'red' section is fine orienteering, with good map contact and accurate compass and pacing.

Traffic-Light Orienteering

Emphasis on running and speed changes. Adjusting your speed to the section of each leg is a strategy which should help you slow down when map contact becomes most important, i.e. close to the control.

Green – the first part of each leg which should be covered as quickly as possible. The detail can be ignored and large features used to maintain contact. Compass and pacing help you run confidently but are not always necessary where there are a lot of map features to 'collect' you. This is *rough* orienteering.

Amber – as you approach your attack point it is necessary to increase map contact, so the pace is dropped to enable the map to be read more frequently and easily.

Red – slow right down, even to a walk to maintain continuous map contact. Pace accurately and keep checking the compass to find the control. This is *fine* orienteering.

Emphasis on concentration and map contact. Focusing on running speed has frequently been the downfall of many a top orienteer. It is a better strategy to use the principle of traffic-light orienteering as described above, concentrating totally on your navigation and not on how fast you are running.

Green – concentrate on picking up the major features, look at your map to keep contact whenever you can without dropping your pace.

Amber and Red – as the control is approached your attention on the map and detail in the terrain should increase. Concentrate on looking carefully at the map and visualising how the ground will look as you move towards the control. Remember: 'The next control is my urgent destination', and 'Think orienteering fast not running fast'.

Fig 72 'The next control is my urgent destination'.

Advanced Techniques

Fig 73 *Continuous map contact used on open fell terrain. The orienteer navigates using a compass bearing with map reading, racing through distinctive features circled on the map. Small hills stand out and are better to use than marshes on flatter ground.*

Continuous Contact – Emphasis on the Map

The orienteer should know where he is all the time. By following natural features on the ground, he can keep contact with his surroundings and relate them to the map. This is one of the most enjoyable ways of orienteering and should produce consistent results. Some speed may be lost for the sake of certainty of position. The best orienteers who follow this system are able to picture and memorise large sections of their route so that they do not have to slow down too often to look at the map.

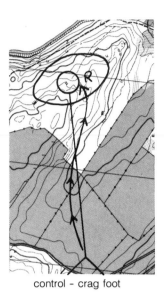

control – crag foot

Fig 74 *Window orienteering. The orienteer arrives somewhere in the 'window', the area round the control. He then relocates and navigates to the control. A good terrain memory will help him remember which way he has come.*

Window Orienteering

This is the 'go and stop' style with emphasis on compass and distance estimation. It is an adventurous approach in which the orienteer runs as fast as possible in the direction of the control. When he thinks he has gone far enough he slows down, relocates and navigates carefully into the control. The ability to relocate quickly involves a highly skilful use of map and compass with a good feeling for relating ground to map.

This system can be adapted by increasing map contact in the first part of each leg. Remember that map contact can be maintained in two ways:

1. Map to ground – look at the map, visualise and remember the features you want to check off. Then look for them as you

Fig 75 *It need only take three or four seconds to punch and run on.*

run through the terrain. This is *map memory*.
2. Ground to map – as you run through the terrain on a compass bearing, watch out for distinctive features which you pass or cross. Glance at your map and identify these features to maintain map contact. This is called *terrain memory*.

Some orienteers will also count paces to keep a check of the distance covered between features, whilst others will use the features themselves to monitor distance. Always keep in mind the four point

sequence at the beginning of this section and allow your own style to develop naturally.

PLANNING AHEAD AND CONTROL FLOW

Another time-saving technique and part of your developing rhythm of orienteering is planning your route for the next leg whilst navigating at speed to the control coming up.

As you punch the control card you have already looked at the route choice to the next control and have decided which way to go. Only three or four seconds have been taken to punch and move on. The last one hundred metres into a control requires all your concentration so the best time to plan ahead is in the first half of each leg at a point where your mind can take a short break from following your route. This is not always easy, especially on a short leg, but must be done if you are going to maintain a good rhythm and flow.

The following actions should be taken in planning ahead:
1. Punch. Re-establish your route as you move away from the control in the right direction. Get going on your route.
2. Look at the code and description for the next control.
3. Plan the next leg as soon as possible.
4. Concentrate on the route and on finding your attack point. Check the code again if necessary.
5. At the attack point concentrate on navigating into the control.
6. As you see the flag or the feature where the control is positioned take a compass bearing to come out of the control. Hold the card ready for punching. If you have a

Advanced Techniques

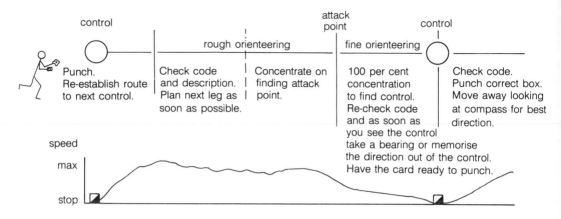

Fig 76   *The recommended sequence for planning ahead and control flow.*

thumb compass readjust it on the map so that it is set for the next leg.

7.   Punch the card in the correct box, and check the code is the one you want. Look at the compass and move off in the right direction.

Control Flow

As you see in the diagram (Fig 76) the orienteer tends to slow down with increased concentration as he comes into a control. He accelerates out of a control moving straight into the rough orienteering phase of the next leg. To maximise the possibility of acceleration out of the control it is recommended that a bearing be taken before the card is punched, while approaching the control.

The whole procedure needs practice and perseverance. Try it out at an event on an easy area where you can spare some concentration to develop the rhythm. If you get it right and use it well, this can increase your speed by at least half a minute a kilometre. Try it and see.

4 Racing

Competitive orienteering is exciting. You go out to match your skills with those of the course planner. Your opponents are the terrain and yourself. Controlling your speed, making good route choice decisions and navigating accurately is the essence of the competition. Your final position and time behind the winner give you a standard to be pleased with or improve upon. The chapters on basic and advanced techniques describe the skills which have to be learned to orienteer. You may want to apply these skills non-competitively (*see* Wayfaring page 112) but the sport of orienteering is navigation at speed. The skills of the game must be tested in the race and assessed by the results. You will only learn how to orienteer well by entering and competing at organised events.

EVENTS

The colour-coded events mentioned in the first chapter are by far the best with which to start. Standards are roughly the same throughout the country and progress can be easily measured. Ten minutes a kilometre is a good standard to aim for at each level if you are going to be competitive. Aim for this sort of result before attempting the next colour.

Badge Events (*see* Event Standards page 115) are the next level of competition and are organised regularly in each region. Here you enter an age group class. Within each age group there are courses for men (M) and women (W) and usually at two standards 'A' and 'B'. These events form the basis of the British Orienteering Federation's proficiency badge scheme with Gold, Silver and Bronze awards available. These are also a good indication of progress.

Badge awards can also be claimed at

Fig 77 The skills of the game are assessed by the results.

57

Fig 78 Boxes of pre-marked maps at the start line of a National Event.

National Events of which there are less than a dozen each year. These events can claim Championship status and should provide a high standard of organisation with a reliable map. Many people will drive the length of the country to race at a National Event held on a technically challenging area. Entry has to be made in advance for the main competition but there are also colour-coded courses which can be entered on the day.

Pre-Marked Maps

Many Badge Events and all National Events will provide pre-marked maps. The map is given to you on the start line. It will have your course over-printed on it, with the control descriptions in a tightly sealed map case. Your control card is separate from this unit and can be attached to your wrist in the recommended way (*see* pages 13–14).

You may be offered a separate control description list in addition to the one in the map unit. Take it, and be prepared to attach it to your wristband in a small polythene bag or with clear adhesive film. Your orienteering will be much more fluent if you can keep your map folded as small as possible whilst thumbing your progress, without continually having to unfold it to search for codes and descriptions.

Fig 79 *International descriptions are easy to learn and understand. Separate description lists should be attached where they can be read easily. The finger attachment for the control card is becoming popular in Sweden. It is easy to make, try it.*

International Control Descriptions (Appendix 3)

Used at National Events, these are an international pictorial or symbolic way of representing control descriptions. They are easy to learn and understand, and a closer look at the feature in the centre of a control circle should clarify any symbols you cannot remember.

RACING STRATEGIES

Through experience and practice you will gradually develop a style as discussed in Chapter 3. However, you will discover that your style is best suited to certain types of terrain and if you are going to race consistently well you should be prepared to adapt your approach where necessary. For example, someone who has had good results 'window' orienteering in areas with a lot of line features will find that their relocation skills are unlikely to work in a sand dune or open fell where 'continuous contact' would be the most successful approach. Some competitions will be held on two or even three types of terrain, each of which will need a different approach. These races require a lot of self-discipline to slow down when running from a fast open area into forest, in order to avoid mistakes.

Juniors between the ages of ten and eighteen will find their courses increase in technical difficulty from 'easy' to 'hard' as

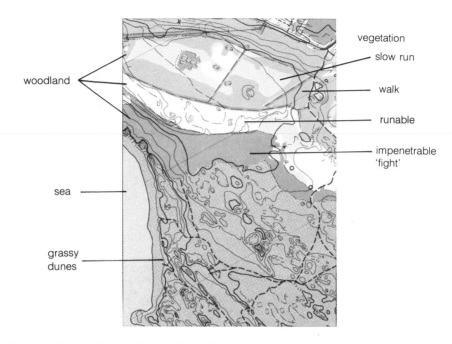

vegetation

slow run

woodland

walk

runable

impenetrable
'fight'

sea

grassy
dunes

*Fig 80   An area with woodland and open dunes. Care must be taken
moving from one type of terrain to the other. The woodland has a
variety of vegetation in it.*

they move up the age classes. Strategies applied successfully on the easy courses will have to be adapted as they become harder. This will be the same for those progressing through the colour courses from yellow to green.

Types of British Orienteering Areas

Flat woodland with a path network. These areas are always fast. Using the line features for route choice saves time. Good control flow with planning ahead will give you an advantage. Any style can be used which maximises speed in the early part of each leg.

Steep woodland. In these areas route choice can be critical. The long path route round

can often be faster than the straight line which may go across valleys and over spurs involving a lot of climbing. Controls on slopes can be difficult to locate. They require a good attack point, especially if you are going down hill. The 'traffic-light' approach should be successful in these areas.

Open areas of fell, moorland and sand-dunes. These areas invite wonderfully fast running. The best routes are usually along the straight corridor between controls. Map contact should not be lost because of the difficulty of relocation, especially in sand-dune areas. 'Continuous contact' or 'traffic-light' approaches are recommended.

Areas with varied vegetation. Forest and re-planted woodland have blocks of young trees and areas of lower runability and

Fig 81   Open areas of fell and moorland are often used for orienteering
events in Northern England.

visibility. These are shown as shades of green on the map. A black dotted line will show the edges of these areas and a distinct vegetation change. This can be used as a handrail or collecting feature as you plan and execute your route. If the green does not have a distinct edge then it is likely to be vague and not even worth considering as an aid to navigation. Areas of green which could be crossed to save distance should be treated with caution. The dark green should be avoided at all costs. There should never be controls in these areas of 'fight'. The lighter greens will vary in their runability and visibility. It is always worth trying to get the feel of how runable these areas are. Do this early in a course before committing yourself to a long route through terrain which might reduce you to a walk. Undergrowth such as heather or bracken and tree brashings can

be almost impossible for the less fit or short-legged!

Racing Strategies for Men

The majority of male orienteers are extremely competitive and like to run fast wherever possible. To gain élite status it is necessary to be very fit, running fast and aggressively throughout the length of a race. Fitness becomes more important after the age of fifteen. The main doctrine to follow at every level is to think orienteering fast, not running fast. Without the self-discipline of keeping your speed under control and main-taining map contact you will find that you will be putting in a lot of unnecessary distance.

In developing a successful racing strategy it is recommended that you start with the 'continuous contact' approach, then as you

Fig 82 Steven Hale, British Champion 1988. Steven has been orienteering since he was 8 years old.

Fig 83 Jean Ramsden. Jean has been racing for Britain for over twelve years.

gain experience and confidence increase your speed in the first part of each leg using a 'traffic-light' approach. You will have to cut corners and take risks but do this when your map reading is good and when you have learnt to relocate quickly.

Racing Strategies for Women

It is encouraging to note that over 40 per cent of orienteers in Britain are female. Despite the mud and the brambles the sport has a great appeal for those who enjoy running but do not want to be compared directly with others on the track or on the road. The necessity for some brain work and a wide range of acceptable physical ability also attracts girls and women.

There are fewer women than men at the élite level in Britain but the group at the top have been generally more successful in world rankings than the men. The top women tend to be in their mid to late twenties when they have had a chance to build up some years of strength training. Confidence, which is frequently lacking in the younger girls, increases with maturity and emotional stability. Some women often reach their full potential in their thirties in this sport, where maximum speed is a small part of the total skill required. If you lack some confidence, even to start orienteering, then enter as a pair and help each other through the initial stages. At whatever level you are competing the strategy of continuous map contact is recommended. There is nothing better for confidence than knowing where you are all the time. Good preparation and control flow should also maximise your talents.

ERRORS

Few orienteers ever run round a course without making any mistakes. The main difference between a good competitor and a novice is the time it takes to recognise that a mistake has been made, and then the time taken to correct it.

Running Too Fast

95 per cent of mistakes made by experienced orienteers are caused by not slowing down enough to read the map accurately. This is likely to result in missing the control. Self-discipline and selection of an attack point can contribute to avoiding these errors. Underrating the difficulty and taking chances at speed can also lead to lost time.

Compass Errors

It is difficult to run accurately on a compass bearing, so the astute orienteer will try to

think of where he could be if he is not following the line he wants. Read the map as much as possible. If you are heading for a line feature, do not be too quick in presuming that you have hit the one you want. Check its direction as you begin to follow it. This sort of concern will also help you to pick up other direction errors such as a 'one eighty'. This is running off 180° to the direction you want. This is more easily done than you might imagine.

Parallel Errors

These are caused when there are two or more similar features lying parallel with each other and along the same line of travel. It can be easy to think you are following the features you want when you are actually following the ones which are parallel. Making this sort of mistake can be very costly in time, because it can take several minutes before you realise what you have done. You can train yourself to be aware of

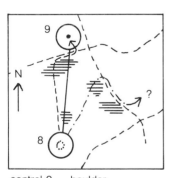

control 9   boulder

Fig 84   A common direction error. The orienteer aims to hit the path, then turn left just before the junction. However, he runs too roughly, does not check the direction of the path and loses time looking for the control in the wrong place. As you run along the path either set the map or take a bearing along the path you want, off the map. A mistake can be spotted quickly.

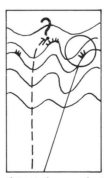
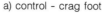

a) control - crag foot   b) control knoll E. foot

Fig 85   Parallel errors. a) The map seems to fit but the runner has picked up the wrong re-entrant parallel to the one he wants.
b) Several parallel ridges on this piece of complex moorland require good map contact and compass skills to avoid a parallel error and the loss of time.

possible parallel errors by looking at a wider corridor of map, rather than just focusing on the narrow line you presume you are travelling along. If you do this, mistakes can be realised early and relocation will be relatively straightforward. The accurate use of a compass will also help to avoid following the wrong features.

Loss of Concentration

This is the reason given for many mistakes, but your analysis should include what it was you did wrong when you lost concentration. For example it is easy to forget how far you have come if you allow your mind to drift away from orienteering. The mistake here is really caused by lack of map contact or not pace counting.

It is easy to lose your mental picture of features leading into a control if your concentration is disturbed by seeing another competitor or even a control not on your course. Other people are a common distraction, and it takes practice and confidence to ignore them and concentrate on your chosen route.

One way of trying to avoid being distracted is to have a word you say to yourself, which acts as a 'trigger' for regaining your concentration. Try a positive word such as 'Concentrate' or 'Contact'. Say it just as you

Fig 86 It is easy to be distracted and lose your concentration.

become aware of the distracting situation. This works best if you can practise visualising the procedure several times before a competition.

Error Analysis

Errors are made by not performing techniques correctly or not using them at all. After each race examine your route, decide which techniques were the cause of your mistakes, and write them down on your analysis sheet. A summary of errors which it is possible to make will be found on the 'Performance Analysis Sheet' (*see* Fig 90).

RACE PREPARATION

The secret to success in race orienteering is confidence and this comes with good preparation and experience. Confidence leads to a relaxed mind which enables good concentration.

One month or more ahead
Look at maps of similar areas and list the techniques demanded by the terrain. Practise those techniques and visualise them. Think about the type of competition.

One to three weeks ahead
Plan travel arrangements and race day routine. Plan the warm-up and train or run at the same time as your start time. Refer to the analysis of your previous two or three races and decide which techniques you need to concentrate on getting right. Read all the information you can about the event. Practise positive thinking about the race and have a positive mental rehearsal.

Fig 87   Concentrate on the race and avoid chattering to people before the start.

RACE DAY

Keep to your planned routine and check through the following points:

1.   Look at the start and finish systems – can you see the last control?
2.   If you have a map, locate and mark the start, the Master Maps, and the finish. Check where north is and in which direction people are leaving the start.
3.   Check the scale of the map and make sure the correct scale is on your compass.
4.   Control descriptions should be easily readable on your wrist. If these are only available after the pre-start, then go prepared with a small polythene bag or adhesive film to cover them, and safety pin them to a wristband. The control card should be waterproofed and attached to your wrist (*see* pages 13–14).

5. Think again about the techniques you want to practise.

Start and Pre-Start

Concentrate on the race and avoid chattering to people unless this is a deliberate ploy to calm nervousness. If a map of the area is displayed, try to pin-point where you are. Keep the body mobile with stretches or jogs on the spot – this can help to keep the mind and body alert.

As soon as you see the course on your map, decide quickly on your route to the first control. Move off, but make sure you know exactly where you are as soon as possible. You should run from the moment the whistle goes but never at the expense of knowing where you are.

During the Race

Here are some tips to remember during a race:

1. Everyone makes mistakes but the best orienteers ignore them and get on with the race. Having decided which route to take try not to change your mind.
2. Try not to be distracted by other people. Have confidence in your own decisions and keep to your own route.
3. Always think about orienteering fast *not* how fast you are running. Even on long path stretches, keep your mind on the race and do not let your thoughts drift to other things.
4. Plan one control ahead all the time and enjoy finding a good rhythm of running, keeping map contact and finding controls.

Fig 88 Move quickly away from the start but make sure you have map contact as soon as possible.

Fig 89 Enjoying finding a good rhythm of running.

5. Be ready for warning signals if the ground does not match the map. Check the compass, look for possible errors and aim to collect the next large feature.

6. Lost? Do not panic. Think logically (*see* pages 27 – 8).

7. Try not to give up completely unless it is near course closure time.

8. It is more difficult to think clearly when you are tired. Be extra careful towards the end of a course or when you have just climbed a hill.

After the Race

Draw in the route you took round the course as soon as possible and estimate how much time you lost on mistakes. Complete a race analysis sheet (*see* Fig 90) and find out the routes taken by competitors who were faster than you. If you had a good race write down how you prepared, what training you did in the few days before it and what was your attitude to the race on the day. If it worked for one race it could work again. The follow-ing race commentary is an example of a 'story' analysis which can be filed with the map.

A Race Commentary

This course (*see* Fig 91) was planned for a National Event to be shared by four classes, M13, M65, W50 and W55. It was 3.6 km long with 125m of climb. It had a technical rating of 4/5 which is harder than usual for the M13s (*see* Event Standards page 115). The fastest time on the course was taken by an M13, a fourteen-year-old boy. He took 42.26 minutes. The slowest few took around two hours. Out of fifty competitors in the four classes only one M13 retired. In this rough, steep terrain only the best orienteers ran faster than ten minutes a kilometre. The winning M13 commented on his route.

Start to Control 1. Clearing east tip (medium difficulty). 'I thought the course looked quite difficult when I first picked up my map but as I got on the move everything just fell into place. The terrain was quite rough. From the start to the first control (the most important one) I thought I would be careful but it turned out to be quite easy.' [Comment – the wall and old fence were used as handrails with the small bridge over the stream as the attack point, less than 50 metres from the clearing.]

Control 2. Re-entrant (hard). 'Having checked my compass I continued onto the track. I ran along, looking to my left for the gap between the thicker trees. I ran up, then along by the wall climbing gradually up the hill. I was lucky to see the control. It was hung low in the re-entrant.' [Comment – careful navigation is needed on a hillside like this. The best attack point would be the re-entrant by the vegetation change 75 metres west of the control. Pace counting would be advisable to stop you going too far.]

Control 3. Small earthwall corner (hard). 'I contoured round the hill following the slope to the earthbank. I saw my control just behind the bank.' [Comment – another M13 found himself on the crags above the earth-bank having climbed without realising it. He located himself on the slope and only lost a few minutes.]

Control 4. Knoll (medium). 'From there I ran up the marsh and through the gap in the trees. The control was much further up and over the hill than I expected. Here I tried to speed up a bit.'

Control 5. Re-entrant (hard). 'I went back through the opening, followed the edge of the trees and went up the hill. It took me a

ORIENTEERING EVENT ANALYSIS AND EVALUATION

Event: .... **Date:** ....

Course: .... **Length:** ....

My Time: .... **Winner:** ....

Total time lost: .... **Mins per km:** .... **Mins per km:** ....

Draw in your route in the map

Summary of mistakes

Leg	What went wrong and why	Est. time lost

Strengths   (What went right today?)

Weaknesses and lessons learned

Other Comments

Look at this before your next event

Fig 90   Race Performance Analysis Sheets. a) A simple event analysis sheet which can be completed after each event and filed with the map for reference. b) A more complex performance analysis sheet useful for identifying and tabulating strengths and weaknesses.

WHY YOU LOST TIME

	Control Number																		
	1	2	3	4	5	6	7	8	9	10	11	12	13	14	15	16	17	18	19
Ran too fast																			
Read map too late																			
Underrated difficulty																			
Took a chance																			
No attack point																			
Did not check features en route																			
Bad route choice																			
Did not follow plan																			
Lacked concentration																			
Followed others																			
Others followed you																			
Disturbed by others																			
Unused to map																			
Unused to terrain																			
Did not read Control Code																			
Did not read Cont. Desc.																			
Tired																			
Did not like map																			
Bad map reading																			
Bad compass work																			
Bad distance judgment																			

ANALYSIS OF PERFORMANCE	Good	Medium	Bad
Concentration			
Route Planning			
Attacking Controls			
Leaving Controls			
Rough Map Reading			
Fine Map Reading			
Rough Pace Counting			
Fine Pace Counting			
Map Memory			
How you managed with the map			
How you managed with the terrain			
Checking Features En Route			
Running Independently			

minute to find the best way through the trees. I followed what I hoped was the ride and was pleased to see the runable forest ahead. I orienteered rather roughly but came upon my control perfectly.' [Comment – this was a risky route and he was lucky to find the ride. The safer way, taken by the winning (and wise) M65, was to collect the ride to the north which led to the 'gap' just above the control.]

Control 6. Re-entrant (hard). 'I ran down the hill to the footpath and went up the wide ride with the ditch running down the middle. I could see the ride starting to drop down the other side of the hill. I turned left but it was early and finished up running through the thicker trees. I knew I had to be over the top of the hill. I hesitated when I thought I had

gone far enough and then I saw the control'. [Comment – at least two competitors made a parallel error here and lost time through not checking the compass on the first part of the leg. They left control 5, climbed the hill, crossed a ride going north instead of west. The ground initially went up and down as expected, but the control did not appear. An M65 then used fast relocation tactics. He ran due north to the forest road, located on the junction and navigated carefully onto number six.]

Control 7. Boulder 1, 5×2.0×2.0 (medium/ hard). 'I decided to go straight down the hill to the next control. The forest, although dark green on the map, didn't seem too thick and it looked as good a route as any. I ran fast on down the hill knowing that when I hit the

70

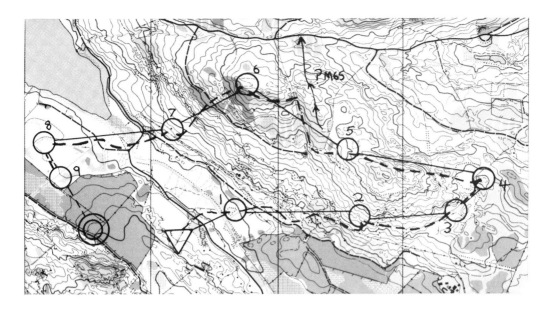

Fig 91 The course and route taken by the winning M13. The alternative
route to control 5 follows a ride through thicker trees. The route to
control 6 also shows how the M65 relocated on the forest road. The
area is a mixture of mature deciduous woodland and coniferous
plantation. The only open area is the finish field.

wall just past number 7 I would be able to go
back to the control.' [Comment – although
the wall is a good catching feature it would
be wise to keep checking the compass for
direction to avoid being pulled too far south-
east.]

Control 8. Ditch junction (easy). 'I now felt
really good so I raced down to the road for
number eight, turned off the path just after
the bend and ran onto the ditch which was
very clear.'

Control 9. Stream (easy). 'I took a bearing to
the last control just to make sure I didn't
mess it up now! I hit it dead on.'

Finish. 250 metres (uphill). 'The run in uphill
was nasty but I managed to run all the way.
I didn't think I had a chance of winning. It
was difficult but everything turned out right
for me.'

Fig 92 'I managed to run all the way . . .
everything turned out right for me'.

A Coach's Comments

This was a good race in rough terrain. This winning run was produced by keeping going and not making any major errors. A high basic fitness level and positive attitude helped him to keep running.

Strengths. Good map reading and contour interpretation skills. A good feeling for distance covered, without pace counting. His route choice is sound but an attack point should always be selected. This would have saved time on controls two, five and six.

Weaknesses. There was no indication in the commentary of planning ahead and I would suggest that at this level of ability he could show further improvement by planning routes one leg ahead, and knowing exactly which way to go out of each control. This planning ahead should be done as early as possible on each leg during the rough orienteering phase.

Pace counting would be an additional skill to draw on. A natural feeling for distance cannot always be relied upon.

Training. Two or three training runs each week and some more technique training will help to build up fitness which will be necessary if he is going to be as successful in M15 next year.

This boy is a member of his region's Junior Squad which has a local weekly session for fitness training. They also meet at weekends for technique training. This squad has organised bus trips to orienteering events in other parts of the country. These extend the experience of the juniors (M/W13–M/W17) as well as providing an enjoyable social outing.

HOW TO IMPROVE

Orienteering can be a frustrating sport. You think you have mastered all the techniques but at every level you will find you make mistakes for which you are not prepared. How do you achieve the 'magic' perfect run?

Fitness

The fitter you are, the less effort it takes to run through the terrain and more concentration can be given to reading the map. A fit body gives an alert mind. Improving your fitness level will guarantee improvements in your orienteering.

Find a Coach

One of the fastest ways of improving is to learn from someone more experienced. Your local club will have a lot of experienced orienteers. Some will be qualified coaches – ask them for help. A coach will shadow or follow you round one or two courses to watch how you orienteer then he or she will make suggestions as to how to develop a good style. He or she will take an interest in how you progress and offer advice and guidance based on a lot of experience.

Race Analysis

The only way to assess your weaknesses yourself is to record exactly what you do during every event you attend. What mistakes did you make and what caused them? Write it all down and file the written analysis with the map with your route drawn on it. At the end of a year you will see that the same cause of mistakes will appear again and again. It may not always be what you were expecting. Having this information gives you a basis for some useful technique training before the next series of events.

Goal Setting

If you really want to improve you must prepare and train for orienteering. Look at the fixture list for the next six to twelve months and decide which events you want to go to and in which of those events you want to aim to perform your best. Whatever level you compete at you want success to get the most enjoyment from the sport. Success should be gained from achieving your goals, not necessarily winning.

These are some suggestions for goals at different levels:

1.   Use the colour-coded events for goal setting, e.g. aim to achieve an award qualifying time in the colour you enjoy running (*see* Event Standards page 115).
2.   Use Badge Events and National Events to aim for the level higher than you can achieve now, e.g. aim for gold standard if you have gained silver.
3.   Aim to be within a percentage of the winner's time.

Try not to set yourself the goal of winning a race – this type of goal is dependent on how other people perform and is out of your control. If you think you are capable of winning or achieving a high place then translate this into performance criteria such as:

I will plan ahead for every control.
If I make a mistake I will just forget about it and keep going.

Fig 93   A future champion? This young girl has gained a Gold Badge award already.

I will concentrate 100 per cent on orienteering fast and not just running fast.
I will aim to run all the way and not stop to walk because I am lazy or tired.

Training

Having set some realistic goals the best way of achieving them is to plan a training programme which includes physical, technical and mental training.

5 Training for Orienteering

One of the attractions of orienteering is the complete demand made on mind and body. However, this means that any training programme should have a balance of physical, technical and mental training elements. At whatever level you wish to improve, it is worth including some of each element into a programme which suits your lifestyle. If you are at school or college then participate in as many running sports as you can. Swimming and cycling will also give you a good start to the basic fitness required to enjoy your orienteering. Technique is best developed through events, club or school training sessions and trying to apply the techniques described in this book. Mental training is just developing the right attitude to races so that you are able to concentrate more easily, making the right decisions and applying the right techniques at the appropriate time. You will find that planned training, however little, will have a beneficial effect on your orienteering and you will enjoy it so much more.

FITNESS TRAINING

Orienteering involves running across country with short pauses and extra efforts, taking between 45 minutes and 1½ hours. It requires endurance, speed, strength and mobility.

The body is an incredible machine which will work at its best when fuelled with the right diet and an efficient oxygen transport system. Oxygen has a critical role to play in the production of energy, and the increase of oxygen (O_2) available to the working muscles is one of the essential objectives of fitness training. By deliberately increasing the heart rate and working the muscles harder than usual, the body will adapt to this challenge and a more efficient system results.

Fig 94 Orienteering requires endurance, strength, speed and mobility.

74

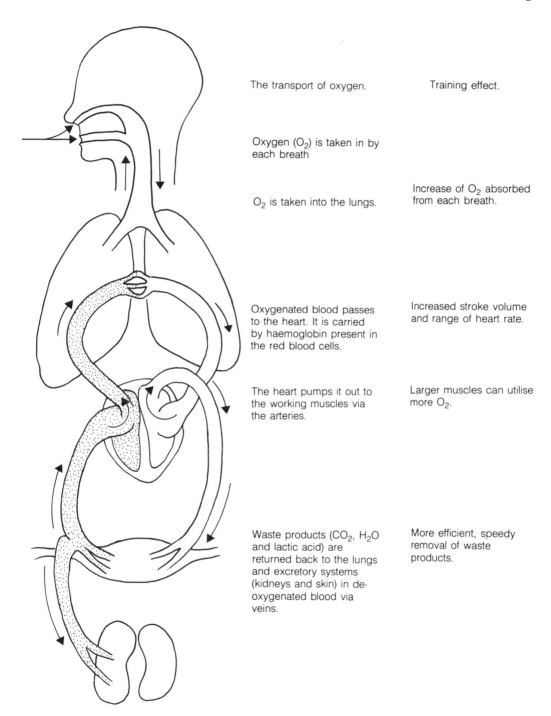

The transport of oxygen.

Training effect.

Oxygen (O$_2$) is taken in by each breath

O$_2$ is taken into the lungs.

Increase of O$_2$ absorbed from each breath.

Oxygenated blood passes to the heart. It is carried by haemoglobin present in the red blood cells.

Increased stroke volume and range of heart rate.

The heart pumps it out to the working muscles via the arteries.

Larger muscles can utilise more O$_2$.

Waste products (CO$_2$, H$_2$O and lactic acid) are returned back to the lungs and excretory systems (kidneys and skin) in de-oxygenated blood via veins.

More efficient, speedy removal of waste products.

Fig 95   A simplified diagram of the oxygen transport system.

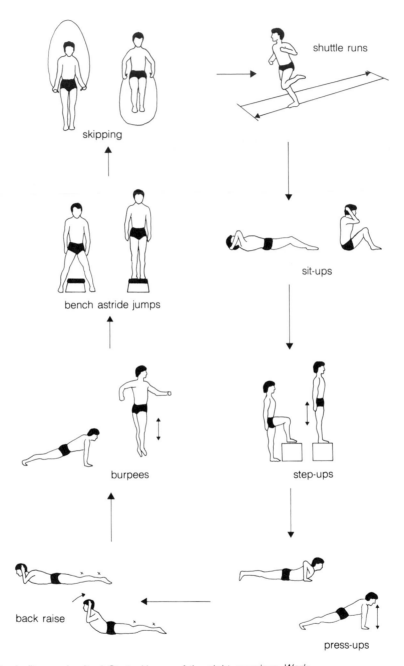

skipping

shuttle runs

bench astride jumps

sit-ups

burpees

step-ups

back raise

press-ups

*Fig 96 A basic fitness circuit. a) Start with any of the eight exercises. Work for 30 seconds on each one. Continue round the circuit. Take two minutes recovery between each of three circuits.
b) Use the same circuit with a partner. Alternately work for 30 seconds on each exercise. One recovers whilst the other one works.
c) No recovery between the three circuits. Record the number of repetitions on each exercise and use these as a measure of your increased fitness.*

General Fitness

Running Training

The first goal to aim for is to run continuously for the length of time you expect to be out on an orienteering course. If this is over thirty minutes, and it usually is, then gradually build up your continuous running time, using at least three sessions each week. In the first week start with ten minutes. Then add five or ten minutes each following week. These guidelines will help as well:

1. Keep off the roads as much as possible. Use footpaths, parks, etc.
2. Find other people with whom to run. Company helps you keep to a plan as well as being more enjoyable.
3. Start steadily and aim to keep going and not to stop.
4. Plan a variety of routes.
5. Take an 'O'-map with you and practise reading it on the run.

If running in pairs:

1. Take a map with a course marked on it.
2. Alternately identify the feature in each control circle without stopping.
3. Look at the route choice for each leg, memorise major features and then tell your partner, without looking at the map.
4. Select an attack point for each leg.
5. Take a couple of running minutes to study the map, then let your partner quiz you on its major characteristics. What is it? Is it flat or hilly? Where are most of the fields, buildings, etc?

This sort of training mixed with other active sports makes an excellent start to developing a routine and making time to run. It will also improve your orienteering. You will not have to walk so often, and you will be able to think much more easily throughout the length of the course.

Circuit Training

A circuit of exercises is another way of increasing your cardio-vascular fitness, and

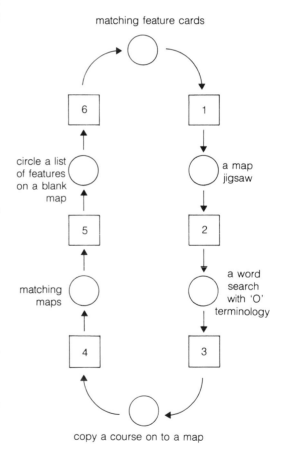

Fig 97 An orienteering circuit. Select six of the exercises from the basic fitness circuit and include a map game between each exercise (see map games pages 101–2). Allow 30 seconds for each game or exercise. Drawing games will necessitate a map for each person.

Fig 98   A slow stretch from the mobility
         section (Fig 114).

Fig 99   Warming up. 'Bum' kicks.

your ability to keep running round your
orienteering course. It is best done with a
group and a leader to time each exercise.
Circuits are very good orienteering training
as they simulate the short pauses and bursts
of effort. Always warm up well before starting a circuit.

Warming Up

If you are going to remain uninjured and
make the most of your training, warming up
should become an automatic part of your
training and racing routine. Your body is just
like a car in that it takes a few miles before
it will run smoothly especially on a cold day.
Wear an extra layer or two to keep the
muscles warm, and include hat and gloves
on cool days. Spend five to ten minutes
jogging to loosen up and waken the body
into activity. Follow this with some slow

Fig 100   High skips.

Fig 101

Fig 102

Figs 101-3   Four warming-up leg stretches.

Fig 104   Stretching before a race improves performance.

stretches selected from the mobility section (page 88). Now run again. This time include some short sprints, high knee lifts, 'bum' kicks and high skips. Some fast running on the spot and final leg stretches should set you up for some strenuous training or a race.

Whenever you have been running hard, an easy ten minutes jogging will help the body to recover faster. Later on, some gentle stretching will stop the muscles contracting and becoming tight.

PHYSICAL TRAINING FOR ORIENTEERING

Once you can see an improvement in your results from some basic fitness training, you can start to become more ambitious. Now is the time to plan your annual training programme and include some specific strength and speed training. A well planned *periodised* programme is designed to give optimum fitness for the competitions you want to do best in.

Your best form will be gained after a period of intensive quality training. This can only be coped with once a high level of basic fitness has been achieved. The period of basic training, therefore, aims to raise your aerobic capacity, that is to increase the efficiency of the oxygen transport system. The body is then able to handle the stresses of hard quality training sessions designed to increase speed and strength for orienteering. You will then be well prepared for racing. Your plan will contain four phases:

1. Basic fitness training.
2. Specific fitness and orienteering technique training.
3. Competition.
4. Transition and recovery.

The objectives and characteristics of each phase are described later in this section after the explanation of how to plan the year's, the weeks' and the days' training.

Planning the Year

Competition Phase

The year plan is constructed by working backwards from each competition phase. You may choose to have one, two or even three competition phases in each year.

First of all decide in which races you want to peak. This decision will be influenced by your goals. For example, someone wishing to attain a higher badge standard would select a minimum of three Badge or National Events as close together as possible. These races will identify the competition phase. The period should not extend over ten weeks as it is difficult to maintain physical and psychological form for longer than this. If you plan to race throughout the year, then select a few races which will be more important than the others. These other races will be used for rehearsal and training. The main races, in this situation, will create two or three competition phases. The following three examples are used to illustrate ways of constructing your year plan.

1. One competition phase of eight weeks taking in the main season's races in April and May.
2. Two competition phases, the first of eight weeks in April and May and the second phase of six weeks in September and October covering the autumn National Events.

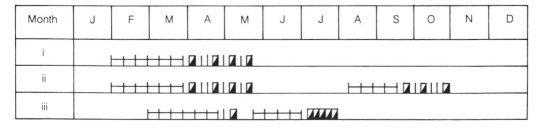

Month	Jan	Feb	Mar	Apr	May	Jun	Jul	Aug	Sept	Oct	Nov	Dec
e.g. i												
e.g. ii												
e.g. iii												

Fig 105 Competition phase.

Month	J	F	M	A	M	J	J	A	S	O	N	D
i												
ii												
iii												

Fig 106 Competition and specific phase.

Training

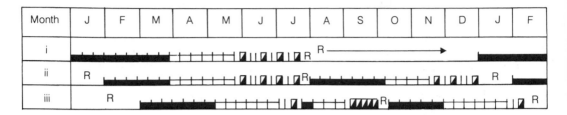

Fig 107   The year plan.

Fig 108   a) A two week cycle of hard–easy training.
b) A three week cycle of easy, medium and hard training.

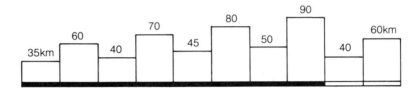

Fig 109   A gradual build-up of distance in the basic training phase.

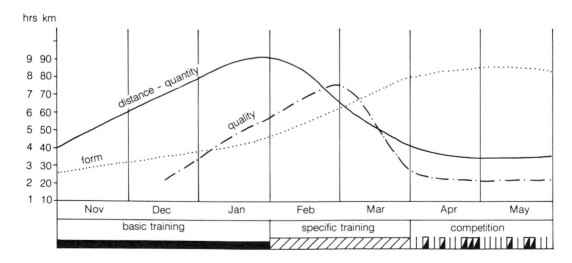

Fig 110   The balance of quantity and quality training in the competition
year. Example; one competition phase in April and May.

3. Three competition phases, the British Championships in May, a Scandinavian multi-day event in July, and the British Night Championships in November.

To allow time to wind down from the hard training, each competition phase should start one week before the first race in the phase or, in the case of single peak races, two weeks before.

Using the three examples, the plan will start by looking like Fig 105.

Specific Training Phase

This is the most important period because it prepares you specifically for orienteering races. It will include some orienteering events which can be used to practise techniques and racing strategies in preparation for the main competitions which follow. A period of four to six weeks should now be identified on your plan. The examples will now look like Fig 106.

Basic Fitness Training Phase

The total distance and time spent training in this phase is the base from which you will race. The period can be as long as eighteen weeks or as short as four. It can also be combined with more specific training if the total time for race preparation is limited to six weeks or less. Now look at the examples in Fig 107.

Transition and Recovery Phase

'R' in Fig 107 represents a period of active recovery where you can give yourself a deserved break after racing hard. It is also a relaxing transition between a competition phase and the next period of race preparation.

Planning the Weeks

Hard and Easy Training

The outline is now complete. The next stage is to plan which will be easy, medium and hard training weeks. This variation allows for recovery and avoids overtraining. It also assists you to plan your training alongside education, family, work, holidays and other time commitments.

Go through the year, week by week, and mark 'E' against all the enforced easy weeks. These would include:

1. The week before a major race.
2. Holidays or periods away involving other activities.
3. Examination or intensive work weeks.
4. Weeks that involve travelling for one full day or more.

An easy week in one phase will not necessarily be the same as an easy week in a later one.

Having identified the easy weeks you can complete the pattern with medium (M) and hard (H) weeks. You can choose to follow a two-week cycle or a three-week cycle, *see* Fig 108. In the basic training phase both the easy and hard weeks will increase in quantity as the period progresses.

The last hard week in the basic training phase should be the one with the greatest distance or quantity of training of any week in any of the four phases in the competition year. To decide the quantity of the hardest week, you first ask yourself what is the furthest distance you have comfortably run in one week. Add 10 per cent to this figure to give you the distance. For each of the hard weeks prior to that, subtract 10 kilometres or 6 miles. You should now see the pattern developing with the quantity of training gradually building up to a peak. Afterwards, the distance gradually decreases, with all the weeks becoming proportionately shorter as more intensive work is included in the specific training phase (*see* Figs 109 and 110). Eventually, you ease off completely for the races in which you are aiming to peak.

Planning the Days

Training Sessions

A training session or training unit is a single practice session with a training objective. Within each phase - preparation, competition and recovery - the training sessions in each week will pursue the demands and objectives of that phase.

The final part of completing your year plan is to write down the training sessions you would include for two weeks of each phase - an easy week and a hard week. Using the recommended sessions from each training phase in Fig 111, select five to ten sessions to make up each week. Keep in mind your target distance (or time), and balance hard and easy days. If you are able to train more than once a day ensure that you allow adequate time for recovery.

It will be necessary to review and update the plan to meet your changing requirements as the year progresses. The information given here should be used as a guide and adapted to fit in with your lifestyle, goals and motivation to train.

Examples of training sessions in each week are shown with the characteristics of each phase.

Characteristics of each Phase

Basic Fitness Training Phase

The aim is to develop general endurance in order to cope with specific training and the races which follow. Your race results will usually reflect the amount of training completed at the end of this period. Putting 'the miles in the bank' gives you a basic fitness from which you can take on a larger load of quality training. It also gives you a sound background fitness which can be built on each year.

Long runs should be done in terrain whenever possible. Events can be used for terrain running training and for practising new techniques. Use this time to plan your orienteering technique training for the next phase. The second half of this phase should include at least two quality sessions each week, one of which should be some sort of hill training such as long hill intervals (LI) or Fartlek. Circuits are excellent for building up aerobic and specific fitness over the winter period.

The hazards to be aware of in this phase include overtraining, too much road running in cheap running shoes, a poor diet and a chilled body caused by standing around in damp training clothes. All these can lead to injury or illness. In the winter months two or more of these conditions can result in a week or so without training which will disrupt your plan.

Here are two examples of weeks in this phase.

Easy week - early part
1. Long distance (LSD)   60–90 mins.
2. Circuit training.
3. Short distance (SD)   25–45 mins.
4. Distance run (LSD)   40–60 mins.

Basic Training sessions	Specific Training sessions	Competition Training sessions
Long slow distance 50–120 mins Distance runs (LSD) 25–50 mins Other active sports Circuit training Orienteering events	Long slow distance Distance runs Circuit training Technique training	Long slow distance Distance runs Technique training
Quality	**Quality**	**Quality**
Short distance (SD) Long intervals Long hills Fartlek Cross country races Fell races	Short distance Long intervals Short intervals Long hills Bounding Short hills Marsh/heather/sand intervals Tempo training Fartlek Special variations Weight training Specific circuits Cross country races Fell races Road races Orienteering races Technique training	Short distance Short hills Short intervals Marsh/heather/sand intervals Tempo training Special variations Fartlek Orienteering races

Fig 111   Recommended training sessions for each training phase.

5. Long intervals (LI).
6. Rest - other recreational activity.
7. Long distance (LSD) 45–70 mins.
(6 sessions)

Hard week - later part
1. LSD   50–90 mins.
2. a) SD   30–45 mins. b)   Circuit.
3. Long hill intervals (LH).
4. a) LSD   30–40 mins. b) LSD   40–60 mins.

5. LI.
6. Rest.
7. LSD in terrain   50–120 mins.
(8 sessions)

Specific Training Phase

This phase aims to develop fitness and techniques specific to the demands of orienteering. This is the most demanding phase including at least three quality

Training

sessions each week. The sharpening of fitness and increase in maximum oxygen uptake capacity cannot take place without the preceding basic training phase. Care must be taken not to overload the training to an extent where there is a negative effect on fitness. This may lead to illness or injury.

This period must include a revision of basic orienteering techniques. Events should be used to refine racing strategies and to develop confidence for the races in which you want to peak. One or two races can be selected as rehearsals where you practise a complete routine of preparation. These should include any mental training exercises which you believe will help improve your concentration. You should also be looking at, and running with, maps of areas with similar terrain to the events in which you will be competing. Finally, it is important to be looking forward to these races, this is the whole purpose of all your training.

Two examples of weeks in this phase are:

Hard week
1. a) Short distance (SD)   30–45 mins.
   b) Circuit.
2. Long intervals (LI).
3. 'O' Technique   40–70 mins.
4. Fartlek   40–60 mins.
5. Short hills (SH).
6. Long distance (LSD)   35–65 mins.
7. 'O' Technique   50–70 mins.

Easy week
1. SD   25–45 mins.
2. Special variation   a) (page 88).
3. LSD with 'O' Technique   40–60 mins.
4. SH.
5. Special variation   b) – pacing pyramid (page 88).
6. LSD   35–60 mins.
7. Competition.

Competition Phase

The aim is to be on form and feel good for the races in which you plan to peak. Remember to start each race determined to think orienteering fast, not running fast. The week prior to each race should be planned carefully and recorded, so that you can repeat or modify a pattern of training which leads to a good race result. If the phase covers several weeks, it will be necessary to fit in harder training in weeks when there is no major race. This should improve or maintain your sharpness. Technique training should aim to correct any mistakes which have been made in races. Thorough analysis of races is important for future planning.

Two examples of weeks in this phase are:

1. LSD terrain run with map   50–70 mins.
2. Short intervals (SI).
3. Technique   40–60 mins.
4. Short distance (SD)   25–40 mins.
5. Tempo training.
6. Rest.
7. Competition.

1. LSD   40–60 mins.
2. Short hills (SH).
3. Technique   40–60 mins.
4. Tempo training.
5. Rest.
6. Short run with a few fast sprints   25–40 mins.
7. Competition or LSD.

Recovery and Transition Phase

This is a period of relaxed training prior to the next period of basic training. Many top orienteers will plan an alternative activity and take a holiday cycling or mountaineering, whilst others will compete in fell races, triathlons or mountain 'O' races. Training runs should be relaxed. The brain should be allowed to rest as well. Time should be spent planning the next year's programme based upon the assessment of your strengths and weaknesses. Determine these from the results and analysis of all your races.

Special Terms

The following are the special terms and types of training which are used in making up a training programme for orienteering.

LSD - Long slow distance. This is running for up to twice race time with a steady heart rate. It is best done off roads, in terrain or on the fells. It trains basic endurance and the body gets used to working for a long time.

SD - Short distance. This is continuous fast running for up to race time, e.g. cross-country races, fell races and time trials. It trains speed and endurance.

LI - Long intervals (aerobic). Run fast for 2–3½ minutes with 1½–3 minutes recovery. Follow this for 1–2 sets of 3–8 repetitions, keeping equal intensity for each run. Repeat over the same circuit or as part of a continuous run. It trains speed and endurance.

Fartlek (speed-play). The athlete is free to adjust the amount of effort and its duration on a continuous undulating run. It trains speed and endurance.

SI - Short intervals (aerobic). Run fast for 10–50 seconds with 10–15 seconds recovery. Follow this for 2–3 sets of 10–15 minutes. It trains speed, and is especially useful on sand, marsh or heather.

Fig 112 Short hill intervals train strength. Female orienteers should include hill work in their training programmes to increase leg strength. Strong legs help to develop speed and clear thinking in rough terrain.

SH - Short hills. Run for 15–20 seconds up a steep hill, using the maximum effort. Jog back for recovery. Follow this for 2–3 sets of 8–10 repetitions. It trains strength.

Anaerobic Training

Anaerobic means 'without oxygen'. The body is challenged to work so hard that the muscles require more oxygen than can be supplied directly via the lungs and heart. An 'oxygen debt' is accumulated together with lactic acid, a waste product which builds up in the muscles. This type of training should not be used by juniors until the heart is fully

Training

formed, by about the age of 17, as it can adversely affect the growth of the heart. However a lot of *aerobic* work will help to make it larger and able to take greater work loads later on.

T - Tempo training (anaerobic). Run for 1–3 minutes using maximum intensity, with 2–5 minutes rest. Follow this for 3–6 repetitions only. It trains speed and endurance and improves recovery rates after hard efforts in a race.

LH - Long hill intervals (anaerobic). Run for 50–90 seconds at maximum speed up a gradual hill. Jog back for recovery. Follow this for 2 sets of 2–4 repetitions. It trains speed, strength and endurance and improves recovery rates.

Bounding - strides with a high knee lift are also beneficial on this gradient.

Special Variations to Develop Speed in Orienteering

a) Find a 1km path circuit. Put out four tapes, one every 250m. Warm up on one circuit. Then run one section fast, one slow, two fast one slow, three fast one slow, four fast one slow, three fast one slow, two fast one slow, one fast. Finish with one circuit to warm down.

b) Plan an 8 to 13km run along paths and tracks. Have 10–15 minutes easy running to warm up, then counting double paces all the time, follow this pyramid sequence. Run for 50 fast 20 slow 20 fast 20 slow, 100 fast 20 slow 20 fast 20 slow, 150 fast 20 slow 20 fast 20 slow, up to 300 fast then down again to 50 fast. Finish with a 10–15 minute warm-down jog.

Fig 113   Flexibility and mobility.

Flexibility and Mobility

Flexibility not only plays a part in warming up the body for any strenuous exercise but it is one of the physical elements necessary to negotiate the forest with ease. Ducking under branches, scrambling over fallen trees, climbing up steep banks and crags require good mobility and management of the whole body. Flexibility exercises should become part of a well-planned training programme.

Your Training Diary

Having planned your training programme, however 'easy', it is necessary and useful to record what you actually did. How far did you run? How long did it take? Where did

Fig 114   A selection of stretching exercises to improve flexibility and
mobility. They can be used as part of a warming-up session or for
daily stretching. The body and muscles should be warm, you
should stay relaxed. Hold each stretch for 15-30 seconds and
repeat at least three times.

Date	Distance (miles)	Running Surface	Moderate	High	Maximum	Steady Run	Continuous Fast	Aerobic Intervals	Anaerobic	Other Training	Strength Training	Orienteering Tech Training	Competitions	Comments
6th	7		25	45		✓								Terrain intervals. 2 + 4 × 3½ mins. 1½ rec. 7min pause. Felt good.
7th	3			25		✓							10	S.F.D. Through woods and fields – mainly paths. + 4 × 30 step ups with weight bar.
8th	8 1		12	1 26		✓								Evening fell race. Good conditions, strong following wind ☺ 8m. 2,700'↑ 4th Beat last years time by 5 mins.
9th	1		30									✓		Put out orienteering controls. Legs stiff from yesterday.
10th	9		30	1 00		✓								Fartlek. 2 × 30 runs on moorland and forest paths. Good warm up + down.
11th	–										✓			Fell walk.
12th	5			20		✓					✓			Long hills 1min, 35 secs, 2½min recovery 5 × 300 metres. (A new session) (run down)
Week's Total:	34		1 37	3 46		5 23								
Running Total:														

Month: June

*RUNNING SURFACE:
R—Roads
P—Paths, grass, etc.
S—Sand, Marsh
F—Fell, Moorland
W—Woodland
O—Other

Specific Training Phase 'Hard' week

WEIGHT: 9st + 02lb

WAKING PULSE:

Robert Bloor 1984

Comments on Weeks Training (if any!): A good quality week. Pleased with fell race! More technique next week.

Fig 115 An extract from an orienteering training diary. It is useful to keep a record of weekly distance and hours to help balance out hard and easy weeks.

you go (on what type of surfaces)? What type of session was it?

By keeping a diary or training 'log', it is easy to follow your programme. You can refer to it in order to repeat sessions which have led to successful races, and avoid those prior to poor ones when you have felt extra tired. Use it to plan the following year's programme, never increasing the quantity by more than 10 per cent. More than this will result in over-training which has a negative effect on your fitness.

TECHNICAL TRAINING

After each race draw in your route on the map and complete a race analysis sheet (pages 68–70). This is the best way to assess which techniques are your strengths and which ones are your weaknesses, unless you are fortunate to know someone who will shadow you and can tell you what you are doing right and wrong. If, for instance, you keep overshooting controls, then you should try pacing in from your attack point. If you get lost as soon as you try to cut corners, then you will need some help with compass bearings and contour interpretation. Once you know why you are making mistakes, you can start to practise the right techniques.

It is quite difficult to set up a technique training session for yourself and this is a good reason for joining your local club and attending organised training days. Initially, orienteering events provide the ideal training ground. There you gradually build up experience and practise applying the techniques

Fig 116 *After each race assess your strengths and weaknesses.*

Training

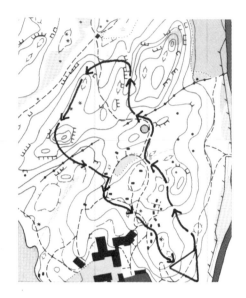

Fig 117 Line orienteering exercise.

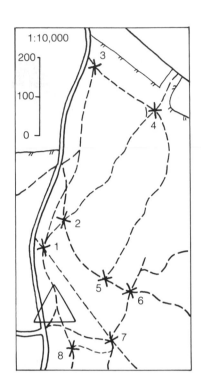

described in this book. You might even consider part of your summer holiday at one of the many multi-day events which take place in July and August both at home and abroad.

If you live near a permanent course or an area which has an orienteering map, then you could plan some of the following exercises to do with a friend. Make sure you have permission to go into the area.

1.   Line orienteering – map reading training, in pairs (Fig 117). Draw a line on the map about 1 – 2km in length linking features which you are able to follow. Follow the line as accurately as possible. In your pair keep alternating the lead. No control flags are needed.

2.   Pacing for good distance estimation (Fig 118). Plan a short route following easy paths. Stop and turn at distinctive features which are an easily measurable distance from each other. Count double paces, and write down the number taken for each

Record of Paces

	Distance	Double paces	
1	150m	70	Run
2	50m	25	
3	350m	158	
4	150m	69	
	700m	$322 \div 7 = 46$	
5	400m	235	Walk
6	50m	30	
7	100m	61	
8	150m	87	
	700m	$413 \div 7 = 59$	

Average run = 46dp
Average walk = 59dp

Fig 118 Pace counting exercise.

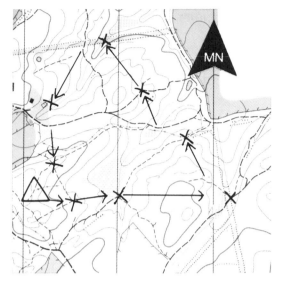

Fig 119 Compass bearing exercise.

section. Walk some and run some. Add up the total distance and paces then work out an average walking and running pace for 100 metres on tracks and paths.

3. Compass bearings or running on the needle (Fig 119). Choose an area with a lot of criss-crossing paths and plan a route to cut across the blocks of woodland aiming for path junctions. See how close to each junction you can be by just following your compass bearing or running at an angle to north. No controls are needed.

4. Relocation – 'Follow John', in pairs. One runner leads the way reading the map, then stops beside a distinct feature. The second runner relocates, decides where they are, then takes the lead and repeats the exercise. The following runner chooses to look at the map while following or only when they

Fig 120 'Follow John!'

Fig 121 Confidence and concentration are linked together.

have stopped to change the lead. No controls are needed.

Some more ideas for technique training:
1. Make your own map of your garden, or of the local park. Then set out a course for your friends.
2. Make sure you know all the orienteering map symbols without looking at the key.
3. Landscape a small area of sand or soil than draw a mini-map of it.

MENTAL TRAINING

Orienteering is not only about being able to read a map and run. The essence of the sport is in making decisions as quickiy as you can and then carrying them out, regardless of what other people around you are doing. This takes a certain amount of cool self-discipline and a lot of concentration. You need to know where you are, where you have been, where you are going and where you are going next. This is not easy when you are trying to run fast as well.

Concentration goes with racing confidence and enjoyment, and these factors are influenced by success. Success is dependent on the goal you set yourself. Set goals which are realistic and which you know you can achieve. For example, aim to be within 30 minutes of the leader, or to check the map is always set before leaving each control. Goals which are dependent on other people, such as aiming to win, are out of your control and rarely help you to concentrate well. If you achieve the goals you have set yourself, then you can really start to enjoy your orienteering and look forward to the next event.

Racing confidence and concentration are linked together and are also affected by other factors which you can control:

1. Good preparation - the better you prepare for an event the more confident you will be.
2. Positive attitude - if you think you can race well you are more likely to be successful, but if you do not think positively it will prevent you running at your best. If you worry about making mistakes and getting lost then you are more likely to do so.
3. Relaxation - if you are nervous then you are tense. Too much tension with anxiety destroys good concentration. The ability to relax is a useful skill.
4. Imagination - practise imagining yourself orienteering well and achieving your goals. It is amazing how this works!

Before your next event set yourself a goal you can achieve. Prepare as well as you can for it and think positively. Warm up well and spend five minutes relaxing and imagining how well you are going to orienteer. Concentrate on orienteering at your best all the time you are out on the course. Finally, enjoy yourself!

6 Coaching

The coach or teacher can help the novice orienteer pick up the basic techniques very quickly, and therefore plays an important role in developing interest and expertise in the sport.

COACHING GROUPS OF BEGINNERS

The two basic concepts which must be taught before anything else are:

1. That the map is the picture of the ground, and
2. That the features on the map must be aligned with the features on the ground, i.e. that the map is 'set' or orientated.

The coach can establish these principles by setting up simple exercises using a room, hall or playing fields. The map should be large-scale, clear and accurate.

Exercise 1

Using a plan of a room or hall, use one wall as north. Place mini-controls (8cm × 8cm) on a variety of fixtures and furniture. The group draw them as control circles on their map. Use the control points for a five-minute score event (Fig 124). A red line on the

Fig 122   The novice orienteers learn the basic techniques.

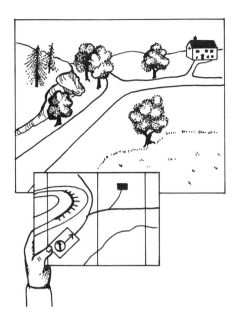

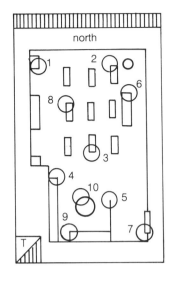

Fig 124   A classroom Score Event.

Fig 123   The two basic concepts which must be taught first. i) The map is a picture of the ground. ii) To navigate accurately the map must be set or orientated.

north end of each map will help the coach see whether the maps are set or not.

Exercise 2

Do this exercise in pairs. Everyone creates a line which is drawn on their room plan. Each person has his own start and finish point. Walk the line keeping the map set then swap maps with your partner.

Exercise 3 – Star exercise

Using a large scale map of playing fields or a park, select a base at a central point where it is easy to set the map by the ground features. Place several controls within 200 metres of the base all on very distinct points. For each control make up two maps with the one control, base, number and description.

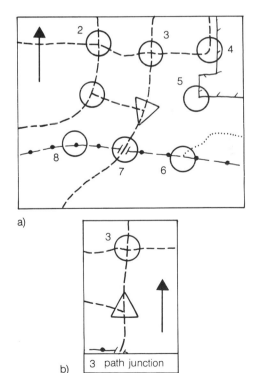

Fig 125   Star exercise. a) A map showing all controls. b) A map with base and one control.

Fig 126   School grounds are ideal for introducing the skills of orienteering.

There should be at least one map for each member of the group. Everyone starts at the base, visits one control, punches or writes down a code letter, returns to the base and changes over maps.

The coach can check anyone who needs help. The group can work at their own pace but always in contact with the coach.

This type of exercise is useful for introducing any new technique to a group. Progress to visiting two or more controls together. The controls can be linked to give a short cross-country course which could be used as an individual course or relay.

INDIVIDUAL COACHING

There are a number of ways a coach can help an individual who wants to progress in orienteering, despite the difficulty of not being able to stand and watch the athlete perform.

Shadowing

The most effective way of finding out how someone orienteers and where their strengths and weaknesses are, is to shadow or follow them round a few courses. You will get a good feel for their style and observe the points where stops and hesitations can be avoided to save time.

Most people are nervous of being watched at first as they do not like to be seen making mistakes, and may try to go abnormally fast to impress you. Reassure them, do not follow too close behind and avoid shouting out comments or instructions as you run along. Afterwards, allow your athlete

Fig 127   Shadowing is one of the most effective ways of coaching.

to explain what he did and defend his mistakes before you say anything. Praise first, criticise constructively later.

Event Analysis

The line on the map showing the routes taken between controls tells a story in itself. The coach should encourage the route line to be drawn on the map after every race. However, this shows little of the thinking and decision making which is going on all the time. To give you this information, a written summary is useful. Completing an 'Event Analysis Sheet' (Fig 90) will help to identify and tabulate the cause of mistakes and will be a good starting-point for discussion.

Discussion

Communication is the basis of all coaching. Use the techniques outlined in this book and ask questions about route execution, distance estimation, and use of the compass. Find out about attitudes to different races. Was there an aim and how much preparation went on? Help your enthusiast to set his or her own goals and draw up training plans. In this way you encourage self-reliance and independence from the start.

Another role of a coach is the ability to set up appropriate training exercises to help practise and improve specific techniques. To gain competence in this aspect it is

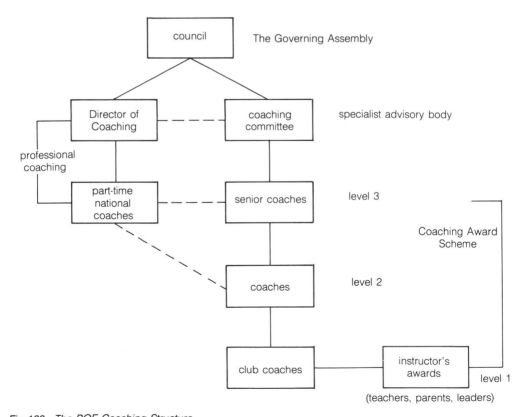

Fig 128   The BOF Coaching Structure.

advisable to attend one of the coaching award scheme training courses organised by the British Orienteering Federation.

ORIENTEERING MAP GAMES FOR THE COACH AND COMPETITOR

Map games are good fun and are an enjoyable way of learning map symbols or brightening up a fitness training session. They can be played sitting down or running, as an individual, pair or part of a team.

Map jigsaws
Paste the maps onto card and cut out into various shapes and sizes. The pieces can be mixed up and made up on a table with or without the original map. Follow this with a running game making the map up at the opposite end of a hall or field carrying one piece at a time.

Matching maps
You will need at least two copies of the same map for this game. Cut out identical pieces from each map and make up two sets of eight. Paste one set on to card and number them one to eight. Use different coloured card for the second set and letter them A to H, in a different order. Put the two sets of cards on the ground or on benches, some distance away from each other. The group, each with a paper and pencil, start in the middle and run backwards and forwards

Fig 129   Map games are good fun. 'What feature do I follow?'

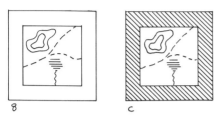

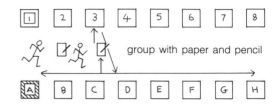

Fig 130   Matching maps.

identifying letters with numbers. This game can also be played like the memory card game, Pelmanism, sitting down. Mix up the two sets of maps upside down on a table. Each player is allowed to turn two cards up at a time. If they match the pair is kept. Who can collect the most matching maps?

Map symbol cards
Make up two sets of cards 3–4cm square. The first set will have the map symbols, the second the names of the symbols. Use contrasting card. Spread them out on a table or put each set at opposite ends of a hall or field or hill. Collect them as you match them. Make several identical sets and work in pairs.

'What feature do I follow?'
Obtain eight to ten maps and plan a 'white' course on each one where each control is linked by one linear feature. Have six to ten control points, using the same number of controls on each map. Work in pairs. One

runs to the map, identifies which feature leads to the first control, runs back and writes it down. The second person runs and identifies the feature leading from control one to control two. Seven controls and a finish will give them four runs each. Change maps and courses and repeat.

PERMANENT COURSES

Many clubs have been instrumental in setting up permanent orienteering courses in town and countryside parks, and Forestry Commission areas. A list of courses in your area can be obtained through the British Orienteering Federation. These courses are ideal for the coach, group leader or individual wanting to introduce or pursue the skills of orienteering.

Anyone can purchase a map pack with all its information on courses and enjoy navigating round controls of their choice. However, the coach should prepare thoroughly if the

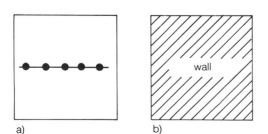

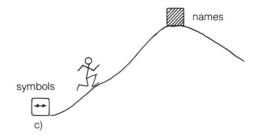

Fig 131   Map symbol cards: a) map symbol b) name of symbol.

0 -1	Road
1-2	Path
2-3	Fence
3-4	
4-5	
5 - 6	
6-7	
7-	

Fig 132   What feature do I follow?

group is going to gain maximum enjoyment from their experience.

First of all visit the area beforehand so that suitable courses can be planned using the permanent control posts. If they are too far apart or difficult to find, extra markers may have to be used to suit the standard of the group. Yellow standard (*see* page 117) is best for beginners.

Protecting the maps with clear adhesive film or a polythene bag will extend their life. Before doing this emphasise the north side with a thick red band, mark on out-of-bounds areas and any useful instructions such as safety precautions. Number each map. There should be one for each member of the group even if they go in pairs. A permanent felt-tip pen can be used on film to link the controls to be visited. This can be wiped off with methylated spirit.

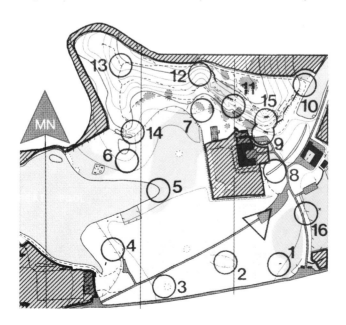

Fig 133   A map showing permanent controls set out in a Midland park.

Coaching

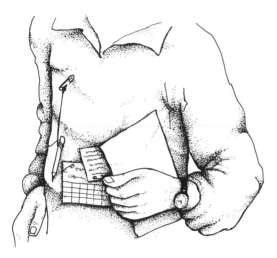

Fig 134   An orienteer organised for copying
codes on a permanent course.
Control card, descriptions and pencil
are attached to the body leaving the
map free to be read more easily.

The control card and descriptions are best attached to the body leaving the map free to be 'thumbed'. A short pencil with string taped to it and safety pinned with the control card will make the code copying process very much simpler. These points of preparation allow the group to be more competitive as well as helping them to focus attention on the map.

Start the session with a map walk to familiarise the group with the area and the map. Establish the scale, the map symbols to be used, how to set the map, and what each control post looks like. Sending young people off without any of this preparation is likely to lead to grouping, getting lost, not finding controls and disillusionment.

Challenges can be presented once individuals have the skills to handle them. Getting lost can be an exciting adventure if you know that you will eventually find your way back.

Coaching should be geared to success and building up confidence. Learning comes through lots of repetition and progressive stages.

7 Course Planning and Map Making

Planning courses is fun for anyone who has access to an area with a map, some control markers to hang out and some friends to find them.

For the coach, teacher or leader it is important to plan courses at the right standard which will therefore lead to success and enjoyment by the participants. Planning courses for beginners is straightforward if the following guidelines are used.

The table of colour-coded courses (*see* Event Standards page 117) provides a useful guide for the planner as well as the competitor. Yellow standard courses are ideal for introducing orienteering to any age group. Even people with some map-reading experience will appreciate a course where they can get used to the new symbols and large scale.

Choose a safe parkland area or woodland with plenty of paths and a clear boundary. The map can be any scale as long as the line features have been drawn clearly. Map scales of 1:5,000 or 1:10,000 allow the untrained eye to pick out and identify these features more easily.

The start and finish should be placed next to each other for ease of organisation and

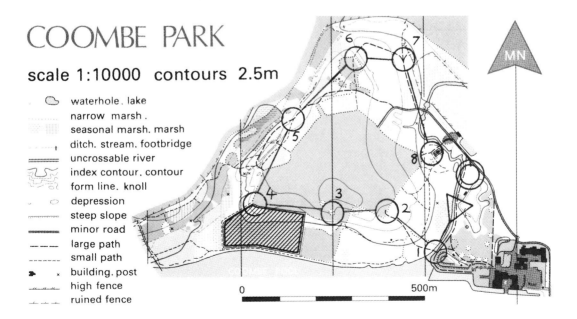

Fig 135   A Yellow standard course.

timing. The start should be on a very distinct line feature, preferably a track or forest road which will lead to the first control.

Controls should be sited on line features or large and distinct features which can be seen and easily identified from the map, for example a monument, a pond or a group of trees in a park.

The control site must be easily identifiable on the ground and be a precise point on the map, for example – 'pond, north end', or 'group of trees, south side'.

Beginners need a lot of controls for reassurance. These should be linked by distinct line features or with only one obvious route choice. One or two right and left decisions are enough at this stage. Older begin-

ners may appreciate a longer course. Keep it at Yellow standard and only make the legs longer than 300 metres if there is an obvious path or track to follow.

The control marker should be hung clearly, never hidden. Orienteering is not a treasure hunt. Control markers hung from garden canes are ideal for making sure they can be seen from all directions. They must be placed in precisely the position shown on the map.

The controls must correspond with the centre of a red circle about 5mm in diameter, drawn on the map. Always use a template for marking maps. If time allows, pre-marked maps help beginners avoid incorrect copying.

Fig 136 Pre-marked maps help beginners avoid incorrect copying of master maps.

Fig 137 *Competitive youngsters will enjoy the sport more if they can run without too much decision making.*

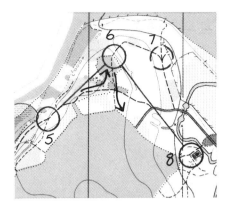

Fig 138 *Avoid 'dog-legs'. Adding a control 7 on this course avoids the dog-leg created by legs 5-6-8.*

Setting the map correctly does not come naturally to most people. It is a skill which has to be taught and practised. The routes will appear extremely obvious and easy to you as the planner but competitive youngsters will enjoy the sport more if they can run without too much difficult decision making.

The next stage in course planning is to offer more route choice as found on Orange standard courses. The theory behind a good route choice is that there are two or more route options which look roughly equal on the map and will take about the same time to run. The straight line option, if there is one, should give the advantage to those orienteers who can navigate well through the terrain. Good map reading should be tested more than compass work, precise distance judgement or fitness.

Avoid 'bingo' controls where finding the control is more a matter of luck than good navigation, for example, a pit in an area of pits or in low visibility. A good orienteer may be within a few metres yet not see the marker. Another orienteer may happen, by luck, to see someone else at the control and not waste any time at all. This is why controls should not be put in areas of 'fight' or where the map is not clear or accurate.

Avoid 'dog-legs' where the best route for competitors is to go into a control the same way as competitors will come out of it. This gives an advantage to those who happen to see someone coming away as they approach the control. These are unfair and should not be used.

Description lists with the codes are part of fair competition. Make these up, using the map key, for each course planned. Keep them concise (*see* Fig 135).

Courses and Maps

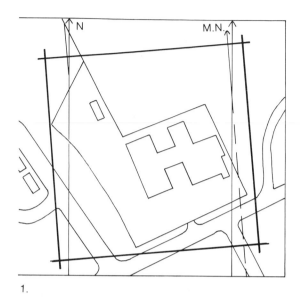

1.

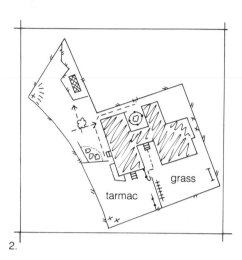

2.

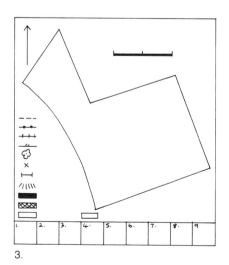

3.

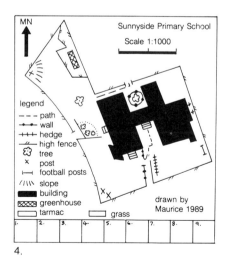

4.

Fig 139   Making a map: 1. Preparation of a base map. 2. Ground survey. 3. Drawing. 4. Printing.

MAKING A MAP

A steady hand rather than a training in cartography is all you need to draw a simple black and white map of a school or recreation centre. These maps are ideal for introducing the sport of orienteering and for establishing basic techniques.

There are four stages in producing a map:

1. Preparation of a base map.
2. Ground survey.
3. Drawing.
4. Printing.

Having made a black and white map it is a straightforward progression to develop your surveying and drawing skills. Larger areas require much more precise surveying techniques. These involve accurate application of compass and pace counting rather than the use of sophisticated instruments. The orienteering map-maker tries to create an accurate picture of the terrain for the competitor running through it. The correct shape and relationship of one feature to another close by is of most concern.

To draw or scribe the map, drawing pens or scribing tools are used to produce correct line thicknesses and symbols according to the International Drawing Specifications. Making a map can be a most satisfying project. It is exciting to see it being used for an orienteering event and it makes excellent technique training for you as a competitive orienteer.

Courses, reading and joining your club map-making team are the best ways to learn more about making maps for orienteering.

8 Types of Orienteering

The most usual type of orienteering is called cross-country orienteering where the competitor has to visit all the controls in a set order.

Relay Orienteering

Relays are a well used variation. With three or four people in a team, each member has to complete a short cross-country course before handing over to the next one. There is a mass start of first leg runners. It is necessary to have slight variations in the courses to prevent runners from just following each other. Relay events are exciting to watch. The first team to finish wins.

The Harvester Trophy which takes place each summer is a relay with seven in each team. The length of courses varies between 3km and 9km. It starts in the middle of the

Fig 140 *The mass start of a relay class at the Jan Kjellstrom Easter Event.
The pre-marked maps are contained in paper bags which can only
be opened at the start signal.*

night so the first three legs are raced in the dark. Over one hundred teams take part with many variations of age and ability.

Night Orienteering

The darker evenings of autumn herald a series of night events throughout the country including British Night Orienteering Championships. Courses are for M/W aged 15 and over and are usually held in open areas where the darkness reduces the visibility. The youngest classes can go in pairs. A powerful head torch is the most useful piece of equipment for these events with the advantage gained by those who orienteer using map and compass and pacing accurately. The best night orienteers run as fast as they do in daylight.

Long 'O'

As the name suggests Long orienteering takes the competitor out for about twice the normal time. A course for M21 would be about 20km. Two or three different areas may be linked together to make a Long 'O'.

Score Orienteering (Fig 141)

The orienteer is presented with a map with up to thirty controls. Each one is worth a number of points. The problem here is to decide how many controls can be visited in the time-limit of one hour and in which order, so as to gain the maximum score. Penalty points are applied to those out for longer than the set time, usually minus 10 for every minute late.

Score orienteering is good for mixed ability groups in familiar areas such as the school playground or local park. Ten points for every control and ten to thirty minutes time-limit are usual adaptations.

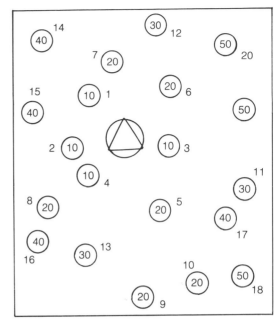

Fig 141   Score orienteering - a limited time to gain as high a score as possible.

Street 'O' (Fig 142)

Many clubs hold a winter series of night street score events. Controls are fire hydrant signs from which the numbers have to be copied. These can be run singly or as a pair. The absence of street names makes this event a real orienteering exercise and a good winter training run.

Norwegian Master Map Events

This is a good way of setting a long course in a small area. At the start, the competitor is only given the first control to copy from the master maps. On arriving at the first control, the second control can be copied from another small master map. At the second control the third is copied and so on until the finish. The course can go close to other controls without the competitor knowing. So

Fig 142   *Street orienteering.*

a small area can be utilised without the possibility of cheating and taking the controls out of order. As a competitor, you have to be ready to copy controls on to your map even in the rain. A map covered in self-adhesive film and a chinagraph crayon is one answer. Tape some string onto the crayon and pin it to you so that it will not be lost. An event like this can also be set up as a training exercise for map memory. No map means you have to remember the whole leg at each control.

Mountain Orienteering (Fig 143)

There are a number of events which are in both the fell running and orienteering calendars. Held over one or two days the courses take you over rugged mountain terrain and are a real challenge to fitness and navigational skills, not to mention survival if the weather is bad. Short and long courses are always available to attract the younger competitors as well as the real mountain men and women. Some of the well-established races are the Lake District Mountain Trial, the Capricorn Event, the Karrimor International Mountain Marathon, and the Saunders Mountain Marathon.

Wayfaring – Recreational Orienteering

Orienteering is a sport for all the family, for there are plenty of opportunities for groups and non-competitive members to enjoy solving straightforward navigational problems in attractive countryside without the pressure of competition. At most orienteering events you can enter a class and choose to be non-competitive. No one will compel you to run.

Permanent courses set up by clubs, local authorities and the Forestry Commission are ideal for recreational orienteers. Map packs can be purchased at nearby information points or shops and a variety of courses are recommended with the instructions on how to get started. This is a good way to get the feel of the sport before going to an event. Information about your nearest permanent course can be obtained from the British Orienteering Federation or your local club.

Other Variations

Cycle 'O', canoe 'O', sail 'O', underground 'O', underwater 'O', pony 'O', ski 'O' – they have all been enjoyed. Combining navigation with physical skills adds another dimension and challenge to various sports.

Ski orienteering is the most organised outside foot orienteering. It has its own world championships in individual and relay racing. Many ski tracks are made in the

*Fig 143   Mountain orienteering – the finish of a Karrimor Mountain
Marathon.*

*Fig 144   Wayfaring – non-competitive
orienteering.*

area and put on the map in green. The problems are more of route choice than in finding the controls. Great Britain's best result in ski-orienteering was a bronze medal in the women's relay in 1975 in Finland. Ski orienteering comes under the umbrella of the British Orienteering Federation.

Appendix 1

British Championships 'Jan Kjellstrom' Easter 2 Day Event	Age Groups 10–70, plus élite (M/W21E).	Advanced techniques for M/W13 'A' classes upwards.
National Events	Age Groups 10–70, plus élite. Entry must be made in advance. BOF Members only. String and colour-coded courses available for entry on the day for non-BOF members.	
Badge Events	Age Groups 10–70. Pre-entry or entry on the day. Badge Award Scheme. String and colour-coded courses often available.	Basic and advanced techniques.
Open/Club Events including introductory events. Usually colour-coded	Colour-coded courses open to individuals, pairs and groups. Club membership recommended after three events.	Getting started and basic techniques.

Fig 145 The British Orienteering Fixtures Structure.

Other Fixtures

There are many other events included in the fixture list each year. Multi-day events, inter-club and schools league events, night events and relays are just a sample of the variety which exist.

Regional fixture lists, which include all the local club events, can be obtained from your club or regional secretary. A national fixture list is always included in the bi-monthly magazine *Compass Sport* (*see* Further Reading page 124).

Appendix 2

EVENT STANDARDS – COLOUR-CODED EVENTS

Colour Awards

A competitor qualifies for a 'Colour' by finishing on three occasions in the top half of those who started the course, or within one and a half times the winner's time. Pairs can qualify for colour awards on white, yellow and orange courses. Record your qualifying times on a record card obtainable from your club secretary. When you have three qualifying times you can claim your colour award.

BADGE EVENTS AND NATIONAL EVENTS

These events are entered according to your age on 31st December of that year. For example, if a girl has her 15th birthday on 3rd July she enters W15 from 1st January of that year. Élite (E) classes are only found at National Events. 'B' classes are available at National Events and, for some classes, at Badge Events. The distance and therefore the winning times for B classes are shorter than for the A classes. For younger classes the B courses are technically easier. String

Fig 146 Courses and classes at a National Event.

Appendix 2

Class	Winning Time	Tech. Diff.	Phys. Diff.	Class	Winning Time	Tech. Diff.	Phys. Diff
M10	20-25	1	2	W10	20-25	1	1
M11	25-35	2	3	W11	25-30	2	2
M13	35-45	2/3	4	W13	30-35	2/3	2
M15	45-55	3/4	4/5	W15	35-45	3/4	3
M17	55-65	4/5	5	W17	45-55	4/5	4
M19	70-80	5	5	W19	50-60	5	4
M21E	80-90	5	5	W21E	60-70	5	5
M21A	80-90	5	5	W21A	60-70	5	4
M35	70-80	5	5	W35	60-70	5	4
M40	65-75	5	5	W40	60-70	5	3
M45	60-70	5	4	W45	55-65	5	3
M50	60-70	5	4	W50	55-65	5	2
M55	60-70	5	3	W55	55-65	5	2
M60	55-65	5	3	W60	55-65	5	2
M65	55-65	4/5	2	W65	55-65	4/5	2

Distances will vary according to the roughness of the terrain.

Level 1 (Easy)

Technical

- controls on line features, usually paths
- controls close together
- no route choice
- routes follow line features

Physical

- minimum amount of climbing
- avoid undergrowth and green areas
- use best available terrain

Level 3 (Medium)   (level 2 between 1 and 3 medium)

Technical

- controls on easier point features
- controls near obvious attack points
- 'catching' line features behind controls
- some route choice but good navigating features
- quickest routes go direct but easier and longer alternatives available
- encourage simple use of contour detail

Physical

- some climbing (not vertical), no extended climbs
- only short distances through green areas

Level 5 (Hard)   (level 4 between 3 and 5 hard)

Technical

- controls on any features but not hidden
- controls far from collecting features but enough detail in control areas for accurate navigation
- errors at controls expensive
- as few controls as necessary for good planning
- legs demanding a range of techniques
- legs across slopes

Physical

- climbing as necessary for good planning
- crossing areas of green acceptable but minimise

Fig 147 Times and Standards.

Colour	Length	Control sites	Type of leg	Technical level	Time for most finishers	Age
String	0.5-1.5km	On the line		Easy	10-15 mins	3-10
White	1-1.5km	Major line features + junctions	Line features No route choice	V. easy	15-40 mins	6-12
Yellow	1-2.5km	Line features + very easy adjacent features	Line features Minimal route choice No compass	Easy	20-45 mins Beginners	8+ Beginners
Orange	2-3.5km	Minor line + easy point features	Route choice Collecting features near control	Med.	35-55 mins	10+
Red	4.5-6km			Med.	50-80 mins	
Green	3.5-4.5km	Small point + contour features	Fine compass and contours More physical	Hard	35-55 mins	
Blue	4.5-6.5km			Hard	50-75 mins	
Brown	6.5+km			Hard	60-85 mins	

Fig 148 Colour-coded Events - standards for competitors and planners.

Appendix 2

courses, novice or colour-coded courses are frequently offered in addition to the age classes, as an on-the-day facility for pairs and beginners. Membership of the British Federation is necessary to compete in National Events. Club members can compete in Badge Events and the colour-coded events available at National Events. Newcomers to the sport are encouraged to join a club after two or three events.

Badge Awards

The National Badge Scheme awards iron, bronze, silver, gold and championship badges after three events have been completed within a time based on the average of the first three in each class. For example, for a gold award your time must be within the average of the first three plus 25 per cent of that average. Silver – average plus 50 per cent, bronze – average plus 100 per cent. The championship badge can only be gained from results at National Events, the British Championships and the Easter 'Jan Kjellstrom' Event. The standard is the winner's time plus 25 per cent. Gold badge standards cannot be claimed by B class runners.

Appendix 3

INTERNATIONAL CONTROL DESCRIPTION SYMBOLS

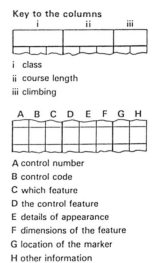

M17A	8.5 km			210m	
1	31	≝			⟲
2	52	↗	•		◔
3	37	⊖	⌣		⚘
4	40	⊓		4	∟
5	49	⊢⊣	▲	1.5	⊙ 🍺
6	75	⬚			
7	32	◈	⊣		
8	54	⊡	•̣		
9	70	∿			

⊙- - - 350m - - -◎ marked route to the finish
350 metres

⊙〉- - -350m - - -◎ 350 metres, marked funnel

|O   350m   ◎| 350 metres, no markings

example: control 5
code 49
middle boulder
height 1.5 metres
north side
refreshments

Key to the columns

i	ii	iii

i class
ii course length
iii climbing

A	B	C	D	E	F	G	H

A control number
B control code
C which feature
D the control feature
E details of appearance
F dimensions of the feature
G location of the marker
H other information

119

Appendix 3

column C

- ↑ northern
- ↗ northeastern
- ± upper
- ∓ lower
- ↕ middle
- • between

column D

- steep bank
- quarry
- earthbank, dam
- terrace
- spur
- rib
- re-entrant
- gully
- dry ditch
- hill
- • knoll
- saddle
- depression
- small depression
- pit
- cliff
- bare rock
- cave
- ▲ boulder
- boulder field
- stony ground
- cairn
- lake
- pond
- waterhole
- stream
- ditch

column D (continued)

- marsh
- small marsh
- firm ground in marsh
- well
- source
- open land
- semi open land
- forest corner
- clearing
- thicket
- felled area
- vegetation boundary
- copse
- road
- path
- narrow ride
- wall
- fence
- footbridge
- building
- ruin
- tower
- shooting platform
- fodder rack
- rock pillar
- single tree
- salt lick
- tree root
- boundary stone
- charcoal burning ground
- anthill
- broken ground
- special feature
- special feature

column E

- shallow
- deep
- overgrown
- open
- rocky
- marshy
- sandy
- coniferous
- deciduous
- end
- bend
- junction
- crossing

column F

- 5.5 height in metres
- 8×3 length/width in metres

column G

- northern side
- northwest edge
- east corner (inside the angle)
- southwest corner
- southern tip
- western part
- upper part (head)
- lower part (foot)
- on the top of
- southern foot
- at the foot

  (direction not specified)

column H

- refreshments
- radio control
- manned control
- first aid

Glossary

Aiming off This is a safe and time-saving navigation technique to find a point on a long feature. It involves deliberately aiming to one side of the point to be found. When the feature is reached there is only one way to turn to find the point. If you have aimed to the left of the point, you turn to the right and vice versa.

Attack point This is an obvious and precise feature within 150 metres of a control. It is used in selecting and executing a route so that the control can be more easily located or 'attacked'.

Badge Event This is a level of event in the British fixtures structure with classes for different age groups. National Badge Scheme awards can be gained at these events.

Base Plate The part of the compass which holds the compass housing.

Bearing The direction in which you want to travel.

Bramble bashers High knee socks with a protective rubber facing.

Class Age classes for men and women, e.g. M13 or W19. Élite (E), A, B and C classes offer a range of distance within some classes.

Cartography Map drawing.

Contact A term used for relating the ground to the map, or the map to the ground, so that the orienteer knows where he is.

Control The control marker or the control site identified on the map as the centre of a circle 5mm in diameter.

Control card This is carried by the orienteer to mark at each control proving that all controls have been visited.

Control code Identification numbers or letters which are displayed at each control marker. Codes are included on the description list to enable competitors to check that they have arrived at the correct control.

Control descriptions Every course has a list of control descriptions giving the features where each control is placed and the codes to be found there, e.g. for control 1 – 1. AZ Boulder, south side. International control descriptions are symbolic and will be found in the appendix.

Control flow An expression used for the fluency of arriving at, punching, and moving away from a control marker. Top orienteers will take 3–4 seconds to do this.

Collect A term used for checking off large features on the route, allowing the orienteer to run fast and ignore irrelevant detail.

Collecting feature A long or large feature used as a checking off point as the orienteer proceeds along his route. It can also be a

Glossary

feature beyond a control, used if the control is overshot. In this context it is also known as a catching feature.

Corridor A narrow band of map or terrain linking controls.

Course The start, controls and finish visited by each competitor. Several different courses are set out at each event. Each class uses a different combination of controls.

Élite (E) The top class at National Events and Championships. Competitors have to justify their ability. A limited number are selected and seeded in the class.

Event An organised competition for orienteers.

Fartlek A Swedish word (meaning speed-play) to describe a running training session over a variety of paths and terrain.

Fight Impenetrable forest, shown as dark green on the map.

Fine compass Used in fine orienteering. Care is taken to follow the compass bearing accurately.

Fine orienteering This is also called precision orienteering. It is accurate and precise navigation. The orienteer knows exactly where he is all the time. Map contact must be maintained. Distance estimation should be precise and the compass followed carefully.

Following Cheating, except when being used as a non-competitive exercise to watch how someone else orienteers.

Form-line An intermediate or 'extra' contour line showing ground detail. Shown by a broken brown line.

Handrail This is a long or line feature used by the orienteer to make his route safe and simplify the map reading.

Index contour Every fifth contour line is drawn heavier to make the height and shape of the ground more obvious on the map.

Knoll A small hill shown by a brown dot, a small brown ring or form-line.

Leg The section of a course between two control points. It also describes the course run by each member of a relay team.

Locate When an orienteer uses the map and the surrounding terrain to find out where he is. Also relocates.

Line features Linear features on the map and in the terrain, e.g. paths, walls, streams, etc.

M An abbreviation for male classes, e.g. M17 (boys aged 17–18).

Master maps These are maps showing the course for each competitor to copy on to his own map. This is usually done after the start, and included in the total time.

Magnetic North lines Shown on all orienteering maps, so that the compass can be used accurately. Magnetic North is slightly west of True North and Grid North.

National Event A British event of a high standard, often used as a championship. Entry is in advance. Pre-marked maps and international descriptions are used.

Photogrammetry The use of air photographs for surveying. Photogrammetric base-maps are drawn from air photographs in a stereo plotting machine.

Pre-marked maps There are no master maps. The map is given to each competitor at his start time, with the course already marked on it.

Pre-start This is your call-up time, usually one to three minutes before your start time.

Punch A pin punch found at every control for competitors to mark their control card. It is a bent piece of strong plastic about 9mm long with a distinctive set of needles at one end. The pattern of needles is different at each control.

Ride A clearly visible linear gap in the forest. A firebreak is shown as a wide ride.

Re-entrant A small valley shown by one, two, or more contour lines.

Rough compass Running on a compass bearing or 'on the needle' without being precise in keeping to the line of travel. Usually combined with rough orienteering.

Rough orienteering The orienteer runs fast, 'collecting' the major features along the route. This can be applied in the first part of each leg.

Runability A description of the terrain in terms of how easy it is to run through it. It is classified on the map by shades of colour.

Scribe, scribing A cartographic technique of producing drawings of each colour to be used by the printer.

String courses Short courses for under tens marked in the terrain by a continuous line of string or series of streamers.

Straight line route This is the shortest route between control points, usually requiring skilful map reading.

Stub Part of the control card which is handed in at the pre-start. It is used to record who is in the forest and for displaying the results at the end.

Terrain Any area away from paths, tracks and roads, e.g. forest and moorland.

Tags Contour 'tags' are short brown lines used to show the downhill side of a contour line in areas where this might be confusing.

Thumbing Holding the map folded with thumb beside location. Your thumb moves when you look at the map, keeping map contact along your chosen route.

Vegetation Whatever is growing in the area of the map will be shown by shades of colour. White is runable trees, green – less runable trees, yellow – open ground and fields (no trees). The boundary between two distinctive types of vegetation is shown by a black dotted line on the map.

Visibility The distance you can see through woodland terrain. Visibility may be good where runability is poor due to undergrowth.

Wayfaring Non-competitive orienteering for groups or individuals not wanting to run in a class. It is gradually being replaced by colour-coded courses.

W An abbreviation for women's classes, e.g. W15 (girls aged 15 and 16).

Further Reading

Bryan-Jones, Gareth, McNeill, Carol, Peck, Geoff, Thornley, Tony, *Orienteering Training and Coaching* (British Orienteering Federation, 1982)
A good all-round book written for the coach but good for anyone wishing to improve.

Compass Sport
The magazine for orienteers. Eight issues per annum.
Subscriptions via the British Orienteering Federation.
Up-to-date news on orienteering and fixture lists etc.

Dick, Frank, *Training Theory* (British Amateur Athletic Board, 5 Church Road, Great Bookham, Leatherhead, Surrey, 1984)
A concise book on all the training elements for any athlete wanting to plan his training more effectively.

Disley, John, *Orienteering* (Faber, 1984)
One of the original books, well worth reading. Interesting extended history of the sport.

Harvey, Robin, *Mapmaking for Orienteers* (British Orienteering Federation, 1985)
The standard book for making maps. Very comprehensive.

McNeill, C., Ramsden, J., Renfrew, T., *Teaching Orienteering* (Harveys, 1987)
The handbook for the teacher, leader or coach.

Palmer, Peter, and Martland, Jim, *The Coaching Collection*, (British Orienteering Federation)
A resource book of tested training exercises and activities.

Railo, Willi, *Willing to Win* (Springfield Books Ltd, Huddersfield HD8 8TH)
One of the best of dozens of books on sports psychology. This is one of the most readable and has answers to most problems that might arise. An audio cassette is also available with the book.

Thornley, Jo and Tony, *Fun with Orienteering* (Kaye & Ward, 1979)
Good for the school library, aimed at youngsters.

Useful Addresses

The British Orienteering Federation, 'Riversdale', Dale Road North, Darley Dale, Matlock, Derbyshire DE4 2HS Telephone: 0629 734042
Information on membership, clubs, permanent orienteering courses, coaching awards, schools schemes and fixtures. Introductory packs for individuals, clubs and schools.

The National Coaching Foundation, 4 College Close, Beckett Park, Leeds LS6 3QH
Courses for coaches at all levels.

Harveys, 12–16 Main Street, Doune, Perthshire FK16 6BJ
Map printing, survey, cartography. Orienteering equipment, books and resources for teachers. Catalogue.

Plas y Brenin, The National Centre for Mountain Activities, Capel Curig, Gwynedd, North Wales LL24 0FT
Courses in orienteering.

Silva (UK) Ltd. PO Box 15, Feltham, Middlesex TW13 6DB
Compasses, orienteering equipment, clothing and shoes. Catalogue.

Suunto, Viking Optical Ltd, Blyth Road, Halesworth, Suffolk IP19 8EN
Orienteering compasses.

'Ultrasport', The Orienteers' Shop, The Square, Newport, Shropshire TF10 7AG
Clothing, shoes and equipment for orienteers. Catalogue.

Index

Other Titles in The Skills of the Game Series

Further details of titles available or in preparation can be obtained from the publishers